MW00614080

Energizers
for Reading Instruction

Richard A.
Thompson

Energizers for

Reading Instruction

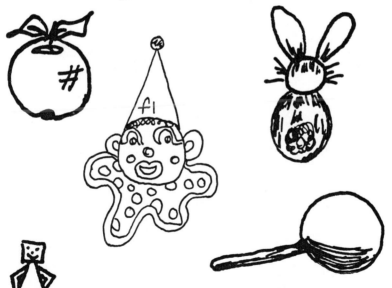

Parker Publishing Company, Inc.
West Nyack, New York

Energizers for Reading Instruction

Richard A. Thompson

© 1973, *by*

PARKER PUBLISHING COMPANY, INC.

West Nyack, N.Y.

Library of Congress Cataloging in Publication Data

Thompson, Richard A   (date)
  Energizers for reading instruction.

  1. Reading (Elementary)--Study and teaching.
2. Reading games. I. Title.
LB1573.T49   372.4'14   72-10892
ISBN 0-13-277228-0

Printed in the United States of America

How This Book Will Help You Teach Reading More Effectively

• • • • • • • • • • • • • •

Ideas assembled in this book have a singular goal—to provide teachers with creative techniques for developing students' reading skills. A viable reading program is vital in meeting varying skill needs of students. It is the individual teacher who is responsible for teaching these needed skills to many students with diverse needs. The games and independent and group activities illustrated in this book will provide reading teachers with flexible techniques for meeting individual and group skill needs of their students.

Creative teachers add zest to their reading programs by using an eclectic approach. They never seem to lack ideas which enrich their basic skill instruction, whatever reading approach is the main course. Creative teaching ideas are the energizers which can enliven any reading program. Helping you, the reading teacher, to become a creative and highly skilled instructor is the purpose of this book.

Experienced teachers realize that learning is most likely to occur when pupils are involved. Therefore, these professionals individualize their reading instruction to meet the needs of their students. By using the ideas presented in this book, teachers can individualize their reading programs to meet specific student needs. Small-group instruction is the most effective means of insuring student involvement in the learning process. This book contains fascinating activities: ideas for games, transparencies, and chalkboard activities. If you use these ideas, you will find that they are highly motivating, yet simple to use. With this wide assortment of creative ideas, you will have flexibility to focus directly on needed word recognition and comprehension skill development.

Though there are a number of approaches to teaching reading, each approach or combination of approaches requires the imagination and resourcefulness of the teacher to present instruction in an interesting and meaningful manner. All teachers, to some extent, are creative; but the most outstanding ones are the most creative ones. Identification of these highly creative teachers is made easy by observing the interest of students. When students are obviously learning enthusiasts, more often than not their teacher is using some creative teaching materials, which are either self-made or commercially prepared.

Teacher-prepared materials take time to make and absorb much thinking time. Teachers seem never to flag in their dedication to giving both in the interests of their students. But time is limited for all, and every teacher is well aware of this limitation. So it is necessary and desirable that teachers have available as many resources as possible. To present replacements or substitutes for the ideas being used presently is not the purpose of this resource book. It is meant to supplement and complement the creativity presently employed.

The wide level of reading abilities and the many specific reading needs of students require the utilization of multi-level reading materials. In every classroom, students vary widely in their reading levels and specific reading needs. Classroom teachers need ideas and materials if they are going to meet the needs and interests of their students successfully. Energizers will help them do that.

If you will flip through this book, you will notice that the contents are graphic representations of creative teaching ideas presented so you will be able to perceive very quickly the ideas and their uses. Where most resource books describe ideas, this book illustrates! Isn't a picture worth 1000 words?

Did you notice that this book contains over 250 energizers? So many may be overwhelming; therefore, I suggest that you try two a week to begin with. After you have become accustomed to using these ideas, you will probably increase your usage as you become more comfortable with your helper.

In planning this book, your author used the reader's convenience as the criterion for organization. Hence, the book is organized specifically to help teachers locate creative teaching ideas and sources of reading materials quickly and conveniently, with explanations being held to a minimum.

If you look at the Table of Contents, you will note that this book has been arranged into ten chapters covering reading readiness, word recognition, and comprehension skills. Basically the arrangement follows the sequential order that skills are introduced in most reading programs, conveniently allowing you to extract activities when needed to go along with whatever reading material forms the core of your reading program. Beginning with Chapter 1, Making Students Ready for Reading, the succession of chapters progresses with ideas for developing vocabulary, phonic skills, structural analysis abilities, dictionary skills, and comprehension skills.

Another convenience to the user is the classification of energizers as being games, group, or independent activities, helping you select ideas to meet your needs. In selecting ideas, keep in mind that many of these could be put on paper for independent or small-group situations, permitting students to work with nominal teacher supervision, either at their desks or at tables.

The energizers in this book have been interspersed without being designated for specific grade levels. At every grade level, teachers have students who have wide ranges of reading achievement and skill needs. Designation of a grade level for a particular energizer would be inappropriate because an idea is useful whenever a student or students have a specific skill need. When selecting ideas, the teacher should choose an appropriate game, group, or independent activity to meet a certain skill need of students.

The last chapter is different in that it includes commercial sources for easy reading series, games, and instructional materials, with publishers' addresses included. Sometimes the principal, PTA, superintendent or someone else will have funds available for purchasing commercial materials. When money is accessible, you may refer to this chapter, surveying what materials are available and from whom. It should be noted that the book series are listed with their readability levels indicated, which is an important factor to be known when ordering these materials. Again, only pertinent information is recorded, in keeping with the criterion of convenience for the user.

The writer's personal experience in teaching teachers and teachers' responses to surveys, indicate that more teachers feel insecure in teaching reading than in any other subject. This resource book was compiled so that teachers will feel confident in teaching reading creatively.

Richard A. Thompson

7

ACKNOWLEDGMENTS

Many people have been helpful on this project and deserve credit. To my many teacher friends who contributed their ideas and helpfulness, I wish to say thanks for your thoughts and energies, for they have indeed added real substance and practicality to this manuscript. I should also like to acknowledge and thank Dr. Donavan D. Lumpkin, my former teacher, who gave me permission to excerpt information from the Ball State Reading Center's Materials Catalog. The information contained in Chapter 10 was drawn primarily from this source.

A very special note of thanks is due Mary M. Fitzpatrick, my sister, for her artistic work and manuscript preparation. It should be obvious to the readers of this book that Mary's talents have made this book aesthetically pleasing.

Finally, Janet, Kim, David and Tim were four good reasons why I enjoyed doing this project. They always keep me happy, no matter what the task.

R. A. T.

Contents

Energizers
for Reading Instruction

1 *Making Students Ready for Reading*

• • • • • • • • • • • • •

Making students ready for formal reading instruction is every teacher's job, although reading readiness skills are most often taught in the kindergarten and first grade. If you are a kindergarten or first grade teacher, this chapter will be of much use to you since it contains a variety of games, group, and independent activities to help you develop the reading readiness skills of your students.

As you know, good visual discriminative ability is a must for reading success. A number of visual discriminative activities are presented for you to use for group instruction and to help you individualize your program in meeting the specific needs of your individual students.

A key to reading success, although sometimes overlooked, is the ability to make sound discriminations. Your students need to develop and use their auditory perception abilities because your students' success in using phonics is dependent upon their ability to hear differences in letter sounds. The auditory discriminations energizers presented in this chapter will enable you to motivate and teach this important reading readiness skill.

Use of the reading readiness energizers presented will enable you to provide an invigorating, exciting early reading program to kindergarten and first grade students, thereby readying them for the formal reading program. Also, other grade level teachers, who occasionally have non-readers, can utilize these activities in making their students ready to read. Enough firm activities are included to challenge all your students who need a readiness foundation.

TITLE: SAVE THE DAISIES   (1)

PURPOSE: To help children learn to associate their small-case alphabet with the large case. It could also be used to introduce the large-case alphabet.

ACTIVITY: Group.

MATERIALS: A. There is a flower for each letter of the alphabet. On one side of the flower is a capital letter, and on the other side is a small one.

B. Two flower pots.

C. A large green worm made out of an egg carton.

PROCEDURE: The teacher will divide the class into two groups, each group having its own flower pot. The object is for one group to gain the largest flower arrangement. The teacher will mix the flowers and hold up one at a time for the groups to tell what the name of the flowers are. First she will call on a student from one group and then a student from the other group, until all the flowers are in the pots. While she is doing this, if one of the students gets the name of his flower wrong, then in the teacher's other hand is a big green worm, and besides not getting the flower he missed put in the pot, the worm will eat another flower out of it. The game continues until all the flowers are in the pots, and the group with the most will win.

ILLUSTRATION:

TITLE: MATCHING CARDS   (2)

PURPOSE: The purpose of this idea is to aid the student in his visual perception and auditory discrimination.

ACTIVITY: Independent.

PROCEDURE: There are two sets of cards: one which is composed of the initial- and final-sound letters and one which is composed of the pictures which depict these initial and final sounds.

The students match the letter cards with the pictures.

ILLUSTRATION:

TITLE: MR. BLOCKHEAD   (3)

PURPOSE: Following directions/visual discrimination.

ACTIVITY: Group.

PROCEDURE: Each student is given the following pieces of paper:

Instruct the class to arrange the pieces of paper to make a man, Mr. Blockhead.

There will be several variations. After allowing the students to experiment awhile, choose one of the student's arrangements that is more logical or realistic. For example:

Then the teacher will tell the other students to arrange their pieces so that they all have a Mr. Blockhead like John's. The teacher may demonstrate the step-by-step construction by arranging her sample pieces on the flannel board, giving instructions as she demonstrates.

1. Place the large square at the top of your desk.
2. Place the large triangle under the square with the point up.
3. Put the two crooked pieces on each side of the triangle for arms.
4. Place the long boxes under the triangle for legs.
5. Place the round circles on the side of his legs for feet.

The student whose arrangement is being used may walk around the class to check the other students' figures to make sure they match his.

This may be repeated using several different students' variations.

19

TITLE:	ZOO ANIMALS (4)
PURPOSE:	To provide practice in identifying the letters of the alphabet.
ACTIVITY:	Group.
MATERIALS:	Twenty-six paper boats with countries written on them. Each must begin with a different letter.
	Use different kinds of animals with names written on them.
PROCEDURE:	The children put animals on the boat whose name corresponds with the name of the country.
ILLUSTRATION:	

TITLE: TELL WHAT IS MISSING   (5)

PURPOSE: The purpose of this game is to help develop visual discrimination skills.

ACTIVITY: Group.

MATERIALS: Several colorful pictures, one envelope large enough to hold the pictures, and one smaller envelope for smaller parts of pictures. Mount several pictures on heavy paper and cut out a major part from each picture.

PROCEDURE: The student will find the missing part of the picture. The complexity of the picture would determine the level of skill.

Choose a leader from the group and have him hold up one of the pictures from the large envelope. The player who correctly tells what the missing part is gets to hunt the missing part in the small envelope.

TITLE: WHAT DO YOU SEE?   (6)

PURPOSE: To help children classify objects commonly grouped by the way they are used—visual discrimination.

ACTIVITY: Group.

PROCEDURE: (1) Have the children name the objects.
(2) Then have a child put an X on the object that does not belong with the others.

ILLUSTRATION:

21

TITLE: ALPHABET MYSTERY (7)

PURPOSE: To build basic letter recognition to help with word attack. Review of alphabet order for older children beginning dictionary and alphabetizing skills.

ACTIVITY: Independent.

PROCEDURE: Give the children a work sheet with an illustration (see below) and have them work it. Tell them if they do it in the proper order they will find a surprise picture.

ILLUSTRATION:

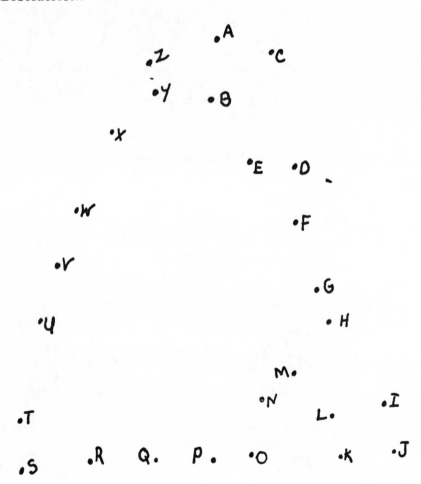

TITLE: ALPHABET SEQUENCE (8)

PURPOSE: To help the child recognize the alphabet.

ACTIVITY: Independent.

PROCEDURE: Each child will be given a picture outline. The children will have to connect the alphabet in order, so that the picture will be formed. When the letters are connected—in order—the picture will be a whale.

ILLUSTRATION:

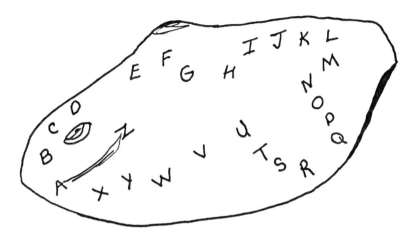

TITLE: THE COMICS   (9)

PURPOSE: Visual discrimination.

ACTIVITY: Group.

MATERIALS: Use any comic strip.

PROCEDURE: Put pictures into a series. Add one picture that doesn't belong. Have the students choose the one that does not belong in the series.

TITLE: MATCHING PICTURES   (10)

PURPOSE: To provide practice in visual discrimination.

ACTIVITY: Independent.

PROCEDURE: Separate two sets of cards containing several pairs into two bundles, with one card of each pair in each bundle. One bundle of cards is spread face up on the table so that each card can be seen. The second bundle of cards is placed in one pile face down on the table. The child turns up one card from this pile at a time and mates it with an up-turned card.

ILLUSTRATION:

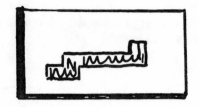

TITLE: CONSTRUCTION LETTERS (11)

PURPOSE: Visual discrimination of letters.

ACTIVITY: Independent.

PROCEDURE: Cut 1½" lower-case letters out of heavy black construction paper. Paste the letters on 3" by 3" squares of shiny colored foil paper. Paste the foil paper on 3" by 3" squares of cardboard. Children can see and trace the letters easily.

ILLUSTRATION:

TITLE: HOW BIG AM I? (12)

PURPOSE: The purpose of this activity is to help develop visual discrimination skills and to aid the development of the concept of shape and size.

ACTIVITY: Group.

MATERIALS: Collect several circles, squares, rectangles, etc., in varying sizes.

PROCEDURE: Have the students arrange the shapes in sequences according to size, starting with the largest circle first, then the next size circle, until they find the smallest circle. Another child can be working with squares, another with rectangles, etc. After the group members get the idea of the game, the shapes could be mixed in a box—then have the students sort them to help develop the concept of shape-size relations.

TITLE: SORTING (13)

PURPOSE: To give the student practice in visually discriminating between objects so that the teacher can be sure he will be able to discriminate letters and words.

ACTIVITY: Independent.

PROCEDURE: Provide the child with an empty egg carton and buttons of different sizes and shapes. Different-colored buttons can also be provided. Let the child sort these in several ways—either by size, shape, color, or number of holes in the button.

After the child has successfully done an exercise like this, he could be given different letters to sort into like piles. If this is done successfully, he can be given similar words such as *was* and *saw* to sort into categories. Capital and small letters could be used to provide for differences so the child would have to discriminate very closely.

Example: Words— SAW
Saw
saw
sAw
sAW
saW

Provide at least three examples of the above words and do the same with the word *was*.

Other words —	Do	Here	Car
	To	There	Far
	So	Where	Tar
	Too	Were	Cat
	Go	etc.	Fat
	No,		Sat
	etc.		Hat,
			etc.

This list could go on indefinitely as long as one letter was changed, two letters were reversed, or one letter was added —and, as long as the child would have to look closely at the word in order to determine which pile it belonged in.

TITLE: RHYMING WORD PUZZLE   (14)

PURPOSE: Sound discrimination.

ACTIVITY: Group.

PROCEDURE: Divide the blackboard into squares. In each square, illustrate two rhyming words. Label one picture in each square.

Children will need drawing paper, pencils, and crayons. Have the children fill in the blanks with the rhyming word that each picture illustrates.

ILLUSTRATION:

26

TITLE:	PICTURE-WORD LOTTO (AUDITORY DISCRIMINA-TION) (15)
PURPOSE:	The game of Bingo can be revised in such a way that it can be used as a game for strengthening certain reading skills.

PURPOSE:

Picture-Word Lotto is designed to help the players gain skill in auditory discrimination by listening to the "caller" pronounce a word and understanding the spoken word. The player can also gain and strengthen concepts by the use of pictures which are to be matched with the appropriate representative word. The game is fun and serves as a motivating force. It can result in a winning player if the teacher desires that there be a winner, and rewards can be offered to the winner also, if desired by the teacher.

PROCEDURE:

Each player receives a playing card similar to the card used in Bingo. Words are used instead of numbers. Each player also has a collection of small pictures which correspond to the words printed on the card. The entire class can play the game, but, in order to avoid confusion, smaller groups of about ten players should be used. The teacher would be wise to allow those students who are experiencing difficulty in auditory discrimination to have plenty of opportunity to play the game. One "caller" is needed to pronounce the words. This could be the teacher or one of the students.

The "caller" pronounces a word which is the same as a word on the players' cards. Not all of the players' cards will have the same words, but each player is given pictures which represent all of the possible words. The player must select from his collection of pictures the one which corresponds to the word. He then tries to match the picture with the printed word if it appears on his card. A player can be the winner when he has pictures arranged in a line across the card or on the diagonal.

AGE LEVEL AND WORD USED:

The game can be used at its best advantage with the primary grades. An adaptation of the game could be used with older children. The pictures could be omitted, and the vocabulary suited to the group could serve as the words used in the play. Words which sound the same could be used, such as the words son and sun. Words which look similar, such as house and horse, could also be used. The above example of words to utilize in the game would be used with the pictures for the primary level.

ILLUSTRATION:

car			
		cap	star
lady	baby	horse	cry
nap		eye	house

TITLE: SOUND PICTURES   (16)

PURPOSE: Sound association.

ACTIVITY: Group.

PROCEDURE: Have the class draw a picture of something that ends with the letter in the box. (Or it could be the first letter of the word.)

ILLUSTRATION:

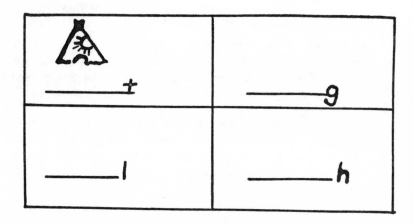

28

TITLE:	LARRY LASSO (17)
PURPOSE:	To provide practice in discriminating beginning sounds.
ACTIVITY:	Group.
MATERIALS:	Flannel board, "Larry Lasso," pictures of objects, and the letters Vv, Ww, Yy, Zz.
PROCEDURE:	The teacher puts "Larry Lasso" on the flannel board along with a picture of an article which starts with Vv, Zz, Yy, Ww. She then calls on a child to come up and pick out the right letter and put it in the center of the lasso.
	Variation—The class may be divided into teams. The team which has the highest number of correct choices wins the game.

ILLUSTRATION:

"LARRY LASSO"

29

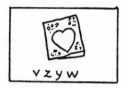
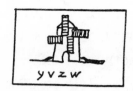

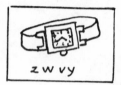

TITLE: AUDITORY BINGO   (18)

PURPOSE: Auditory discrimination of letter sounds.

ACTIVITY: Group game.

PROCEDURE: Make several Bingo cards with letters in the squares. Call out a list of words by which children can identify the beginning letter by its sound. If the children have that letter on their cards, they place a marker on it.

ILLUSTRATION:

WORDS

apple
water
gate
pipe
jump
milk
dog
key
log

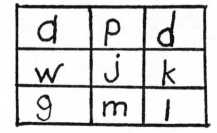

30

TITLE: RHYMING   (19)

PURPOSE: To provide practice in identifying rhyming words for listening skill development.

ACTIVITY: Group.

PROCEDURE: The teacher should prepare on cards, or on the board, a series of two-line rhymes that she can read and show to the class. She should leave off the last word of the rhyme and let the children try to identify the word. This can be done as a game with competition between teams or among students, or it can be done on an individual basis with each child writing the correct response.

> Example: Look, oh, look
>   At my new _____ . (Book)
>   Hippity hop!
>   I just can't _____ . (Stop)

TITLE: RHYMING WORDS   (20)

PURPOSE: To develop auditory perceptions with visual acuity.

ACTIVITY: Group.

MATERIALS: Flannel board, cards printed with rhyming words and some non-rhyming words. The teacher would have a set of cards (a different color) which would have a word to use for rhyming a particular ending.

PROCEDURE: Pass out all cards to the group except the teacher's deck. The teacher puts a word on the flannel board and the children having a rhyming word hold up their hands, then each would place his card under the main word. This goes on until only the non-rhyming words are left. The group can be divided into teams.

ILLUSTRATION:

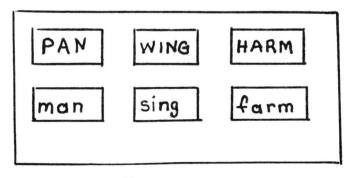

TITLE: PICTURES AND CONSONANTS   (21)

PURPOSE: Auditory discrimination of beginning consonants.

ACTIVITY: Group or independent.

PROCEDURE: A. Given a chart with four pictures across in a row, the students are to say the names of each picture and choose the number of the picture that begins with a different consonant. The student will write the number of the picture that was different.

B. Each row of pictures can be done as the child distinguishes between various beginning consonant sounds.

ILLUSTRATION:

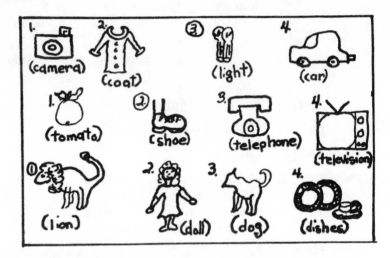

Variations

A. If done as an individual lesson, each child could be given a ditto sheet on which he could circle or star the picture with the different beginning sound.

B. If done as a total class involvement lesson, the class as a group could hold up cards with the correct number of the picture with the different beginning consonant sound, or each picture could be color-coded and the child could hold up the corresponding color card for the correct picture.

Note: On actual chart, pictures are *not* labeled with names and correct number is *not* circled.

2 Guiding Sight Vocabulary Growth via Group and Independent Activities

• • • • • • • • • • • •

Every teacher is concerned with his student's vocabulary growth, for word power creates reading power. Since vocabulary development is such a big area and because it is so important, two chapters are devoted to this topic. In Chapter 2, you will find energizers useful for teaching to groups and energizers which can be used by students independently. Vocabulary game activities are presented in Chapter 3.

Developing sight word vocabularies is the quickest method a teacher can use to make students independent readers. The energizers presented will help you enlarge your students' sight word vocabularies so that they will not only be able to identify a large number of words on sight, but also will know their meanings.

In developing sight word vocabularies, several methods are frequently and successfully used. These methods are incorporated in these energizers. Teaching homonyms, synonyms, and antonyms are productive ways of increasing vocabulary power. The presentation of phonograms and adding the initial letter or letters is another technique useful in stimulating word growth. Since many words have multiple meanings, working on definitions is productive in raising vocabulary strength. These and other ideas are presented to aid you in teaching and strengthening your students' word power.

Many of the illustrated energizers will be helpful to you in providing group instruction. These creative ideas for group instruction will facilitate your preparation of exciting vocabulary-building lessons. Other energizers are for independent work. For example while some students are meeting with you for their group instruction, an independent energizer such as "Expanding Vocabulary" or

"New-Word Puzzle" could be used by the other students on an independent basis.

Whether you need a group vocabulary lesson or independent activities, you will find highly motivating ideas in this chapter.

TITLE: LOAD THE FIRETRUCK   (1)

PURPOSE: To aid word recognition.

ACTIVITY: Group.

PROCEDURE: To help with word recognition, a teacher could go over a group of words with all the students and then divide the children up into small groups to determine how many words were actually learned as she went over the words. Reward a student for recognizing a word correctly by letting him put the flash card on which the word was written in a specially designated place.

Use a firetruck as a place for the boys to place their cards. The cards would serve as fuel for the truck. For the girls, you could use a doll with a slit in her mouth. Both of these things, the firetruck and the doll, would be made out of cardboard and have special slits for the cards. The cards could serve as food for the doll. It would become quite a game among the students to see how many cards they could deposit in the slots.

ILLUSTRATION:

TITLE: LEARNING OF RHYMING WORDS (2)

PURPOSE: Word building.

ACTIVITY: Group.

PROCEDURE: Make a transparency as illustrated. Use overhead projector and ask group to make words using the clues.

ILLUSTRATION:

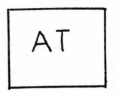

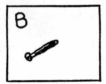  

TITLE: NEW-WORD DEFINITIONS (3)

PURPOSE: To increase word power and give reinforcement to new words studied in other subjects.

ACTIVITY: Group.

PROCEDURE: Divide pupils into two teams, five on each team. A list of definitions are to be given on a billboard. Choose one child at a time from each group to come up and take a card which will have a word on it. This word will match one of the definitions on the billboard. Have the child read the word to the class (with his back to the definitions). Have him look for context clues first, then sound the word out, and finally try to make a definition. After he does this, he may go and see if he can find the definition on the billboard. If he does well in his presentation, he will receive a point for his team.

ILLUSTRATION:

Showing kindly interest and goodwill
Not showing or receiving care
Means of support: necessary for life
The act or process of producing something
To concentrate one's effort in a special activity
Compactness or crowding together of parts
The quality or state of being free
Something placed for safekeeping
To be physically at ease
Not capable of being forgiven

careless		deposits		densely

specialize		manufacturer		independence

comfortable	friendly	unforgivable	livelihood

TITLE: SHOOT THE MOON   (4)

PURPOSE: To build and review sight vocabulary.

ACTIVITY: Group.

MATERIALS: (1) Flash cards with words printed on them.
                     (2) Chalkboard and chalk.

PROCEDURE: (1) Introduce the activity with a short discussion on astronauts, landing on the moon, etc.
                     (2) Draw the illustration on the board (see below).
                     (3) Tell the children that they are going to shoot for the moon by reviewing the words.
                     (4) Go down the row and let each child read the words to try and shoot the moon. Three misfires and you miss the moon.

ILLUSTRATION:

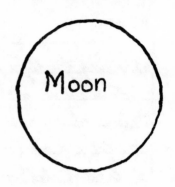

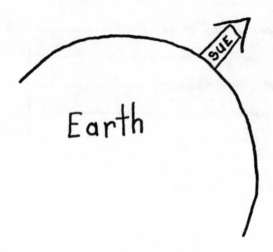

TITLE:	OVERHEAD PROJECTOR EXERCISE	(5)

PURPOSE: The object is to show the many words which can be made by adding the first letter to the same combination of letters.

PROCEDURE: Go through the alphabet one letter at a time. Discuss each combination as it appears as to whether or not it makes a word, and if it does, what its meaning is.

MATERIALS: One transparency set up thus:

slot   slot
 2   1

——   ——

——   ——   _____(line)

Two transparent strips, one with capital letters, one with small letters.

ILLUSTRATION:

```
A          a
B          b
C          c
D          d
E          e
F          f
G          g
H          h
I          i
J          j
K          k
L          l
M          m
N          n
O          o
P          p
Q          q
R          r
S          s
T          t
U          u
V          v
W          w
X          x
Y          y
Z          z
```

TITLE: FLOWER WORD GAME   (6)

PURPOSE: Building words.

ACTIVITY: Group.

PROCEDURE: Using flower cutouts, the children can add the letters on the petals to the letter or letters in the center to make new words. The centers and petals can be made from felt, with different letters to be attached to each. The children actually build the word and then identify it.

39

ILLUSTRATION:

TITLE: GETTING TO KNOW WORDS   (7)

PURPOSE: "Getting to Know Words" can be used to help children learn and become familiar with words that are hard for them. These can be made with white stiff paper, and any words that are giving them trouble can be put on them.

ACTIVITY: Group or teams.

PROCEDURE: Put words that the children are having trouble with on each side, after you have fitted the sides to make a 12-sided figure. The children then take turns rolling this figure. Each child should say the word that shows after the figure comes to a stop, make a sentence using this word, give the meaning, or do something that would help him to know that word.

The children, after awhile, will want to make up their own game.

ILLUSTRATION:

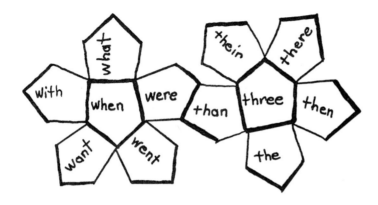

TITLE: HOMONYMS   (8)

PURPOSE: To differentiate between several homonyms from context sentences.

ACTIVITY: Group.

MATERIALS: Flash cards for students; teacher makes sentences.

PROCEDURE: Pass out flash cards; the teacher reads the sentences; the child with the correct card stands.

The context sentences containing homonyms (the correct one) are illustrated by the child who has the correct card by standing at his desk.

ILLUSTRATION:

FLASH CARDS

Written in Green   Written in Red

PEACE   PIECE

TITLE:	KEEP THE RED BARON AWAY (9)
PURPOSE:	Sight vocabulary drill.
ACTIVITY:	Group.
PROCEDURE:	The teacher and pupils all sit around a reading table with Snoopy's Red Baron in the middle. Place five- to eight-word cards in front of each pupil with the word side down. The teacher says, "This is the Red Baron who will try to win all of your cards. He would. like to keep you from learning your words, but you can beat him." The first pupil on the right of the teacher turns up his first card for the class to see. If he can pronounce it, he can keep it turned face up. If not, he must give it to the Red Baron.

The Red Baron can be made of construction paper or, if possible, obtain a stuffed Red Baron which is now on the market. |

TITLE:	SIGHT WORD IDENTIFICATION (10)
PURPOSE:	To drill and stimulate interest and knowledge of sight words.
ACTIVITY:	Group.
PROCEDURE:	Use a flannel board. Make a background with colored chalk. Use pictures of familiar objects to create a scene. Let the children identify as many of the objects as possible with words written on small cards. Place the cards on a small bulletin board next to the flannel board. Allow the children to come up one at a time and place a word card on the flannel board next to the picture of the object it names.
ILLUSTRATION:	

TITLE: PHOTO-WORD   (11)

PURPOSE: To develop word power.

ACTIVITY: Group.

PROCEDURE: Have the class cut out pictures of things like animals, objects, or people. Then, with the class, make up stories using the pictures in place of some words. When the story is finished, list these words on the board and have a student go up to the board and write the appropriate word under the picture.

The  said, "Whooo is there?"

owl

TITLE: INTRODUCTION TO HOMOPHONES   (12)

PURPOSE: To learn that a homophone is a word which although it sounds like another is spelled differently and has a different meaning.

ACTIVITY: Group.

PROCEDURE: Introduce the word *knot* by writing it on the board after getting your students' attention by trying to tie a knot while they watch. Ask them what it is you are trying to do, and when they respond that you are trying to tie a knot, ask how the word is spelled and write it on the board.

Then ask for the spelling of the missing word in the sentence, "Please do_____ tie another knot." When they reply *not* put it in the blank you have provided on the board. Introduce the words *write* and *right* in a similar fashion and the words *to* and *too*.

Having introduced these three, tell the students that all the words that are like the pairs on the board are called "homophones" and direct them to practice in identifying them.

Culmination Activity: Ask the students before turning to the assigned pages, to answer, by raising their hands, the true or false question: A homophone is a word that sounds like another but looks like and means something different.

TITLE: ANTONYM SPIN (13)

PURPOSE: To review antonyms.

ACTIVITY: Group.

PROCEDURE: Construct a wheel out of paper. Put an arrow on the wheel that will spin around. Divide the wheel into sections and write a word in each section. Divide the class into two teams. Select a person to spin the arrow and a person to keep score. Have one child from each team go to the blackboard. Then the spinner spins the arrow. As soon as the arrow stops on a word, the children at the board turn and write the antonym of the word the arrow stopped on. The first child to finish writing the correct word is the winner and wins a point for his team. The game continues until each player has had a turn. Then the points are tallied and the winning team declared.

ILLUSTRATION:

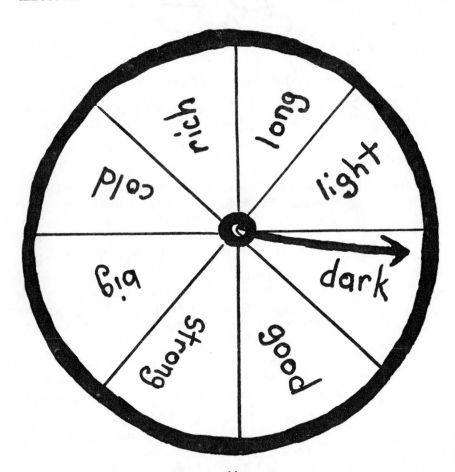

TITLE: CAN YOU CROSS THE BRIDGE? (14)

PURPOSE: For pronunciation and definition of new vocabulary words.

ACTIVITY: Group.

PROCEDURE: Build the bridge with vocabulary words. Each student will "step" from one word to another, pronouncing each word and using it in a sentence, before moving to the next word. Each word must be pronounced and used in a sentence before the student has successfully crossed the bridge. The bridge could be made up of phonics or any type of vocabulary aid desired.

ILLUSTRATION:

TITLE: HOMONYM SPINNER (15)

PURPOSE: To develop skills in recognizing and using words with similar sounds and confusing meanings.

ACTIVITY: Groups or teams.

PROCEDURE: Make a disc approximately 1 or 2 feet in diameter and divide it into ten sections with a spinner in the center. Choose five different words that have homonyms which give fifth graders the most trouble. Mix up these ten words and place them in the ten spaces on the wheel. The words should be placed on the wheel with tape or something else which will enable you to replace the learned words with new words.

A child spins the spinner and then must tell the meaning of the word on which the spinner landed. Teams can be formed and certain classroom privileges can serve as prizes.

ILLUSTRATION:

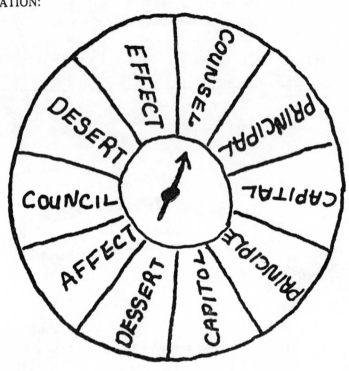

TITLE: TWINS   (16)

PURPOSE: To help students with visual discrimination.

ACTIVITY: Group or individual.

MATERIALS: Two sets of cards which contain like creations; the number of pairs can vary depending upon the teacher's discretion.

PROCEDURE: To start the game, sort the cards into two stacks, with one card of each pair in each stack. One stack of cards is spread over the table face up. The child then proceeds to turn the second stack face up, one card at a time, placing the like cards together. The teacher should check the student's work before allowing another student to start the game. An example of two cards of like design are below.

46

ILLUSTRATION:

TITLE: NUMEROUS NAMES   (17)

PURPOSE: Increase word power.

ACTIVITY: Group.

PROCEDURE: Name as many words as you can, beginning with a given letter in a limited period of time.

Examples:

(b)	(1)	(w)
baby	light	winter
bottle	laugh	warm
ball	like	wet
blanket	lemon	witch
birth	letter	worm
banana	list	wonder
bird	little	wood
bunch	Llama	watch

TITLE: KNOWING ANTONYMS   (18)

PURPOSE: To develop understanding of antonyms.

ACTIVITY: Group.

PROCEDURE: Pictures of opposites, boy and girl, are put on construction paper and taped on the board. The teacher states sentences with one antonym in each, and the students finish the sentences with the other antonym. When the children think of the pair of words, they write the antonyms under the picture. The teacher states these sentences:

1. Candy is sweet, but pickles are _____ .

2. An airplane is fast, but a horse is _____ .

3. The sky is above, the ground _____ .

4. A cat runs on its legs, but a car runs on _____ .

5. In the morning the sun rises; at night the sun _____ .

47

ILLUSTRATION:

Girl

Boy

TITLE: ASSOCIATING WORDS WITH PICTURES   (19)

PURPOSE: To teach sight words.

ACTIVITY: Group.

PROCEDURE: Draw a background scene on a flannel board and cut out pictures so they can be changed to suit the story or the specific needs of the children.

This activity can be used as a game, with the class or group divided into two teams. Each team takes turns and places the small cards with the words on them next to the picture of the thing on the board. The team who places the greatest number of word cards on the board wins the game.

TITLE: PICTURE STORY   (20)

PURPOSE: To develop an understanding of the order of events, create logical thinking patterns, and express creativity by expressing in written form what they see happening in the pictures. Could also develop left-to-right eye coordination, organization of thoughts, and an endless variety of creativeness, depending on the age of the class or ideas of the teacher.

ACTIVITY: Group.

PROCEDURE: Make up a series of pictures, each depicting an action that would tell a story if arranged in proper order. These pictures are cut apart and given to the students, who arrange them in proper sequence and paste them to their papers. They can then write their own story about what is happening in the pictures. The students could even compose their own storybook. After completing the books, the students could exchange them and read each others' books.

OTHER: They could also be used from the first grade on up to higher grades by variation and degree of difficulty, according to the age and ability of the student. There could be different uses in one classroom.

ILLUSTRATION:

TITLE: DOES IT RHYME? (21)

PURPOSE: To reinforce learning of the meanings of words they have been introduced to in their lesson.

ACTIVITY: Group.

PROCEDURE: On large cardboard cards, print the reading words introduced for that day. On smaller cards, write words that rhyme with them. Place the large cards in the chalk tray so the group can see them. Give each student five of the smaller cards. When a student finds a card he thinks will rhyme with the reading word, he takes it to the board to check similarities or compares the two from his seat. He then pronounces the compared words for the teacher, who marks a point for his team if his verbal comparisons match.

ILLUSTRATION:

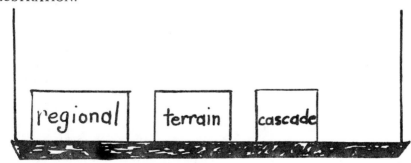

TITLE: SIMILE UNDERSTANDING   (22)

PURPOSE: Understanding similes.

ACTIVITY: Group.

PROCEDURE: Students will orally make up a sentence using a simile, to compare different types of things.

Motivation:

Student participation of describing one person to another using the words "like" or "as."

Material Needed:

Cards with an adjective, verb, or adverb, then the words "like" or "as."

Example:

light as a _____ .

sweet like _____ .

black as _____ .

Activity:

The teacher hands out cards—as in "Example." The student will make up a sentence containing a simile, using the card.

Evaluation:

Student makes the sentence to the teacher's satisfaction.

TITLE: DAZZLING DEFINITIONS   (23)

PURPOSE: To increase word power and provide practice in listening for a definite purpose.

ACTIVITY: Small group or class.

MATERIALS: Chalkboard, chalk, and a list of definitions of words.

PROCEDURE: The group is divided into two or more teams. A list of words for which definitions are to be given orally is written on the chalkboard. The teacher or leader reads the definitions, and the players on each team take turns giving the corresponding word. If a player misses or cannot get the answer, the other team gets to play. The team with the most points is the winner.

Adaptations:

(1) Two or more definitions could be given before a team gets to answer. The words must then be given in the same order as were the definitions.

50

(2) To make the game more difficult, the list of words could be omitted from the board.

(3) For independent seatwork, the children could make definitions to be used in the game.

Cautions:

(1) Give the definitions only once.

(2) Choose words which will enrich the children's vocabulary.

TITLE: CREATIVE ACTIVITIES (24)

PURPOSE: Some words sound alike but look different and have different meanings (homonyms).

ACTIVITY: Group.

MATERIALS: Heavy paper and a felt pen for marking a set of cards (you make) with homonyms.

PROCEDURE: Two to six players. Cards are shuffled and dealt out in rows, face down. The first player turns over two cards. If they "match," the player keeps them and takes another turn. If not, he turns them face down and the next player tries to match two cards. The player with the most pairs (pears) wins the game.

ILLUSTRATION:

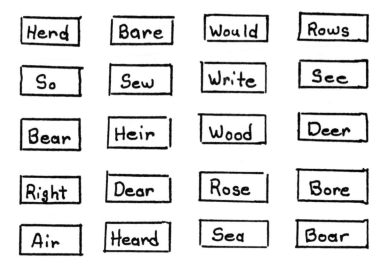

51

TITLE: EXPANDING VOCABULARY (25)

PURPOSE: To develop word power.

ACTIVITY: Independent.

PROCEDURE: Children add names or descriptions for these things as they find them in their reading.

ILLUSTRATION:

1. rose
2. petunia

1. trail
2. lane
3. highway

1. large
2. comfortable
3. strange

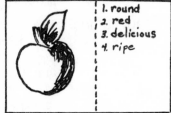
1. round
2. red
3. delicious
4. ripe

TITLE: WORD BUILDING (26)

PURPOSE: Word building using a vicarious experience.

ACTIVITY: Independent.

PROCEDURE: A miniature barnyard scene is a form of giving children a type of vicarious experience. Take a small piece of plywood and glue some fake grass on the top of it. Leave a place for a painted lake and corral. A small barn and animals can be bought at a dime store.

Place the display in the back of the room and allow the children to play with it. They will talk with each other about the animals. In a few days, the teacher can develop a game by using flash cards. Place an animal on a card and have the children look and then say the word. Gradually, they will try to place the card on the right object.

ILLUSTRATION:

TITLE: FLOWERS FOR YOU! (27)

PURPOSE: To help children build and review sight vocabulary.

ACTIVITY: Independent.

MATERIAL: Large piece of paper for each child. Flower pot for each child with bare stalk growing from each pot. Flower with new vocabulary words on it.

PROCEDURE: (1) Have children construct flower pot and paste it on their own large piece of paper.
(2) Review new vocabulary each day. As child correctly reads new word, give him a flower with that word on it to be pasted on his bare stalk.

ILLUSTRATION:

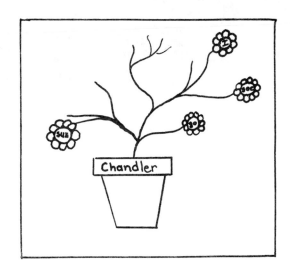

TITLE: CROSSWORD PUZZLE (28)

PURPOSE: Word drilling and vocabulary expansion.

ACTIVITY: Independent.

PROCEDURE: Crossword puzzles are always an effective way of drilling students on words they should already know, but they can also be used to teach students new words. For instance, when you are beginning a new story in their reading book, you can incorporate the new words from the story into the puzzle. They should be placed so that the words they already know will provide clues to the new words. A word list should be given to help the students spell the new words.

New Words

space
planet
rocket
eave
bolt

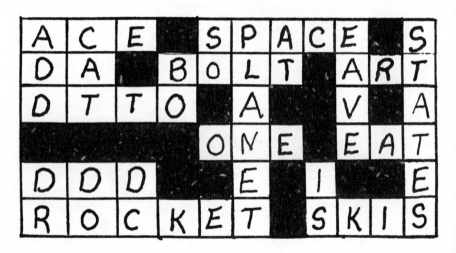

3 Enlarging Reading Vocabularies Using Games

• • • • • • • • • • • • •

The enrichment of children's vocabularies is an objective of teachers at all levels, for reading power increases in relation to vocabulary growth. This chapter will help you meet that objective in a fun way because it contains many exciting vocabulary-building games for your students.

As you know, motivation is a prerequisite for learning. By using these games, you need not be concerned about lack of motivation on the part of your students, since the games themselves contain intrinsic motivation. Even the titles are "attention getters" and are bound to arouse the curiosity of your students.

Whether you need a game for a small group or a large one, you will have a number of different, pleasurable games at your fingertips in this chapter, providing you with the flexibility necessary to meet individual pupil needs.

Let me give you a tip. When I taught in elementary schools, occasionally visitors would come in, sometimes without advance notice. Parents, supervisors, administrators, even foreigners, came to see what kind of a program was being carried on. Of course, every visitor couldn't witness a novel or exciting lesson by just dropping in, so I planned a few activities to have on hand, some of which are in this book, guaranteed to excite my students. And whenever I needed a stimulus for my pupils to perform with learning enthusiasm, I ran in a new game plan. I think you would agree that beats running students to the board for arithmetic drill, which a colleague of mine used to do.

Flip through this chapter and see the many ways these games can help you provide a stimulating vocabulary-building program.

TITLE: WORD LINGO GAME   (1)

PURPOSE: To develop recognition of sight words.

ACTIVITY: Game.

PROCEDURE:
1. Run off a ditto with 25 blank squares.
2. In the center put the word *free*.
3. This game is similar to the game Bingo.
4. The teacher calls out the word and each child puts down a marker to cover his word. (Allow time for the children to read their cards.)
5. Bottle caps work well as markers and can also be used later as math counters.
6. If a child does not know the word, then allow another child to show him what the correct word looks like.
7. If no one knows the word, then the child can see how to spell it that way.
8. If the child finds a new word, then he is learning a new sight word for his sight vocabulary.
9. If he already knows the word, then he is practicing his word recognition skills.
10. By using a blank ditto, the teacher can write in any words she wants to stress or have the children review.
11. To win the game, the child must be the first one to get a whole row of words covered—either horizontally, vertically, or diagonally.

ILLUSTRATION:

Go	Girl	Can	Come	Why
Ball	Look	Bat	Out	Bad
You	Run	**FREE**	To	My
What	All	Red	Is	Want
See	With	Of	He	And

TITLE: PLANET TICKET GAME   (2)

PURPOSE: Sight vocabulary drill.

ACTIVITY: Game.

PROCEDURE: Each child has a word card (planet ticket). He must show his "planet ticket" to the astronaut (chosen leader) before

57

he goes on board the space ship. When the astronaut calls for the child's "planet ticket" (his word), the child must get off the space ship.

ILLUSTRATION:

TITLE: GUESS THE WORD (3)

PURPOSE: The purpose of this game is to teach word extensions and vocabulary.

PROCEDURE: Show these definitions with an overhead projector and have the children guess what word fits each one.

		Answers—
1. A head that glows.		1. Headlight
2. A head the football player knows.		2. Headgear
3. A head that pains.		3. Headache
4. A head that gains.		4. Headway
5. A head that marks the dead's remains.		5. Headstone
6. A head that's food.		6. Headcheese
7. A head for the printer.		7. Headline
8. A head that is center.		8. Headquarters
9. A head that every woman shows.		9. Headdress
10. A head that seats the crowd for dinner.		10. Headwaiter

1. A hand for the acrobat.	1. Handspring
2. A hand for the monkey.	2. Hand organ
3. A hand for the criminal.	3. Handcuff
4. A hand that's for play.	4. Handball
5. A hand for the creative.	5. Handicraft
6. A hand for letters.	6. Handwriting
7. A hand you often spoil.	7. Handkerchief
8. A hand that's good looking.	8. Handsome
9. A hand for the bike.	9. Handle bar
10. A hand that supports.	10. Handrail

TITLE: THE ASTRONAUT AND MISSILE CONTROL (4)

PURPOSE: Word recognition.

ACTIVITY: Game.

PROCEDURE: Two children (from each team) are chosen. One sits in a chair (Missile Control), and the other child stands behind the chair (astronaut). The teacher has made flash cards of several review spelling words, and also of several new words. The teacher shows the cards to the two pupils. If the astronaut says the first new word correctly before Missile Control, he remains standing. The child who misses goes back to his seat. The team that says the words correctly gains 1 point. This can also be done using word definitions.

ILLUSTRATION:

TITLE: HOMONYM RUMMY (5)

PURPOSE: To learn homonyms (synonyms or antonyms).

ACTIVITY: Game.

PROCEDURE: Write homonym word pairs, one word on each 3 x 5 index card. In lower left-hand corner, write a small number from five to ten, in accordance with the level of difficulty of the words.

Students play the game like Gin Rummy. Each player gets seven cards; he then matches any pairs and lays them on the table in front of him. Students take turns drawing cards from a stack on the table, until one player has matched all the cards in his hand. The first player to match all pairs, wins the game. The player with the most points wins.

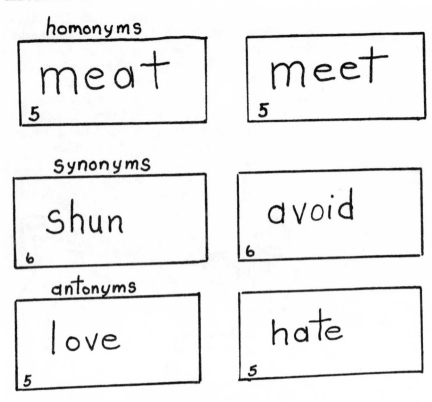

TITLE:	CARROUSEL WORDS (6)
PURPOSE:	The purpose of this game is to enforce sight vocabulary and word recognition skills.
PROCEDURE:	This game can be played at any level of the elementary school; only the variation of words used is the necessary change. I recommend this game for two to four players.
MATERIALS:	Poster paper with a design similar to the one on the facing page; a spinner; different markers for each player.

Players spin to see who goes first. The first player then spins the numeral spinner again and moves the number of spaces indicated. He must read the word that he stops on. If the word is mispronounced, then he moves back to his previous space. The first player to circle the board two times is the winner.

Teachers can use many variations for this game, such as substituting the words for definitions.

ILLUSTRATION:

Carrousel Words

(Board spaces: listen, village, skillet, Cabbage, go back 4 spaces, basket, FREE SPACE, Maine, Scene, main, mane, glove, brother, avenue, fasten, STARTING PLACE, collar, collar, almost, circus, pair, pear, pier, dollar, move ahead 2 spaces, borrow, merry)

TITLE: THE WORD-SPINNER GAME   (7)

PURPOSE: Making new words.

PROCEDURE: This can be made on a large piece of poster paper. Start with one child. Turn the dial until it stops. It will land on a big letter and a small letter. The object of the game is to make new words. The child must start the word with the big letter and must have in the word the small letter. Each section is marked with points—if the child is able to make a word successfully, then give him those points and an extra 2 points if he knows what it means. This requires a lot of thinking.

This would also be good for use in math. Substitute the big letters with numbers 10, 20, 30, 40, 50, and 60. Let the small letters be numbers between 1 and 9. Use it for addition or multiplication.

Example: The dial is on Big R and little d—such new words could be:

read	ready
red	reed
rode	remainder

Make each section a different color and try to make your sections even. You can also substitute the letters for any that you might want to use.

Explain that the capital letters are used to indicate which letter is used to begin the words, and all but proper nouns should begin with small letters.

61

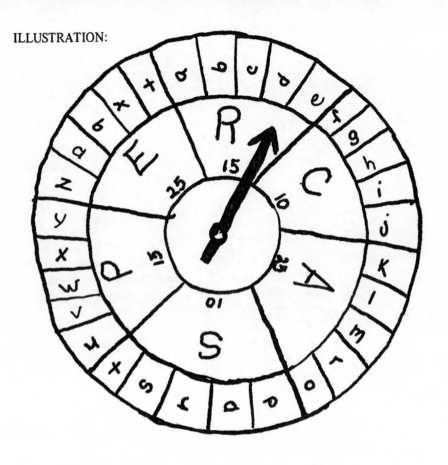

TITLE:	STORY BINGO (8)
PURPOSE:	To gain in word recognition.
ACTIVITY:	Game.
PROCEDURE:	Each child is given a "bingo" card on which approximately nine words are written. Each child is also given nine cover slips of paper to black out the words. The teacher reads a story containing these words. As each word is read, the child who recognizes the word blacks it out with his cover slip. If the child blacks out three words in a line, a column, a row, or diagonally, he says "Bingo." The winners are allowed to do something special (i.e., go to recess, take a break). The game is continued until all of the children are winners.

"The BLACK CAT was sitting....

~~Black~~	plant	cow
~~Cat~~	Water	Go
See	Look	Green

TITLE:	MARCH ON DAISIES	(9)

PURPOSE: To give the child practice reading words that he has learned.

ACTIVITY: Game.

PROCEDURE: This is a game for about six children to play at one time. The children have a game board with squares marked off with red and blue daisies. The board also contains sayings such as "stop," "go back one space," etc. There are cards with blue daisies on the top which also have vocabulary words from the children's reading. The other stack of cards is marked with red daisies, and each card has a character from a story on it. There is a dial which the children spin for a number. They move the number of spaces they spin and draw a card according to the space they land on. *Example:* The child lands on a square marked with a red daisy, and he chooses a card from the stack with the red daisies. He then has to pronounce the name of the character on the card. The game proceeds until a child reaches the finish square and is declared the winner.

ILLUSTRATION:

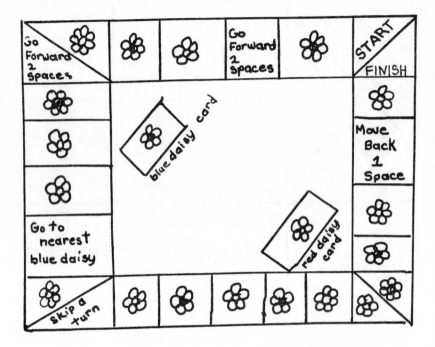

TITLE: MAILMAN   (10)

PURPOSE: This game is for enrichment. This activity could be used for those who have finished their assignments ahead of the others.

ACTIVITY: Group.

PROCEDURE: Place transparency on an overhead projector and have the children transcribe the following letter:

ILLUSTRATION:

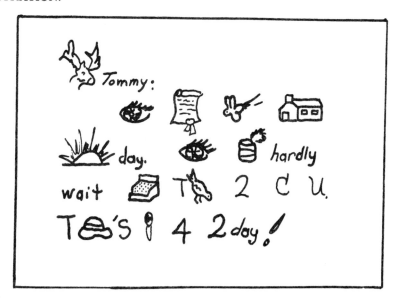

(Dear Tommy:
   I will be home Sunday. I can hardly wait till then to see you.
That's all for today!)

TITLE: NEW-WORD TRAIN   (11)

PURPOSE: The purpose of this game is to aid the children in word
           recognition.

ACTIVITY: Game.

PROCEDURE: Place the word train on the chalk rail. Pronounce the words
           for the children. Let them say the words. They may keep a
           card if they can say the word.

ILLUSTRATION:

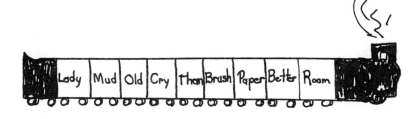

TITLE: I AM THINKING   (12)

PURPOSE: To develop vocabulary and increase listening power.

PLAYERS: Two or more.

PROCEDURE: The leader starts by saying, for example, "I am thinking of a word which means about the same as unhappy." The other players guess in turn by saying, "Is the word sorrowful?" Whoever guesses the word becomes the leader. (To avoid trouble, have the leader write the word secretly on a piece of paper.)

Adaptations:

    (1) The players could be divided into teams and points given for correct answers.

    (2) Instead of synonyms, antonyms could be used.

Cautions:

A referee may be needed to determine the correctness of an answer.

TITLE: SIGHT WORD GAME   (13)

PURPOSE: To develop word form clues and meanings.

ACTIVITY: Game.

PROCEDURE: In this game, the child can match the word with the picture (word form clue). One side of the word card has the word in capitals, the other side has it in lower case. The teacher can have the child match the picture with either the lower case or the capitalization of the word, or both. This way the child not only becomes familiar with the word itself (meaning), but also with what each case looks like, whether it be capitalized or in lower case. The child can also see what letters ascend and which descend (the visual structure).

Along with this, the teacher could make up some sentences such as *"This is a dog."* or *"There is a cat."* and have the child match the sentence with the picture.

ILLUSTRATION:

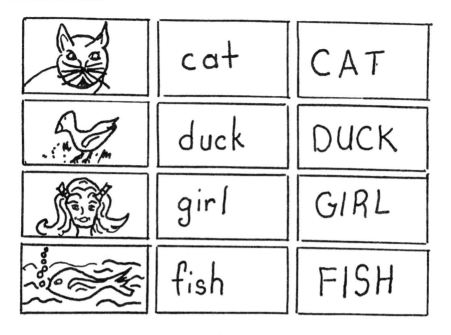

	TITLE:	A PICTURE WORD GAME (14)

TITLE: A PICTURE WORD GAME   (14)

PURPOSE: To aid word recognition.

ACTIVITY: Game.

PROCEDURE: The teacher should pick out vocabulary words which can be illustrated by picture cutouts. To play this game, you need to make bingo-type cards with 25 squares on them. The vocabulary words are written in the squares. The teacher then calls out a word and shows the children the picture that is on her set of cards. The children place their buttons on the word. Five correct covered words in a row wins the game, providing the child can pronounce the words that he has covered up.

ILLUSTRATION:

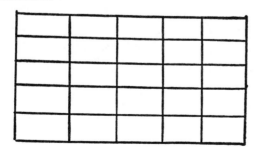 

TITLE: WORD-OBJECT GAME (15)

PURPOSE: This exercise is for motivation and to instill in the children the concept of a word with an object. It could also be used as readiness experience for reading.

ACTIVITY: Game.

PROCEDURE: Each student, not knowing what it is, will have a picture of an object on cardboard placed on his back; i.e., a big house with the word HOUSE written on it. The children will work in groups, and each child will stand up in front of his group with his back to the rest so they can see the object while the others give him hints. After each student has guessed his object, the class will review just the words without the objects.

TITLE: WORD-SPIN GAME (16)

PURPOSE: This game is to encourage children to learn new words and use them in a sentence. It will help the teacher find out if children know the meanings of words.

ACTIVITY: Game.

PROCEDURE: This is a game that children can play in small groups. A child spins the wheel and picks a circle from the pile corresponding to the color that came up on the wheel. The child makes up sentences in which he could use the word, but he leaves the word out. Others in the group have to guess the word.

MATERIAL: (1) Spinner with four different colors on it.
(2) Colored circles, with words appropriate for the grade level written on them.

ILLUSTRATION:

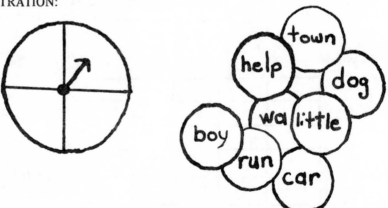

68

TITLE: GOING PLACES–DOING THINGS   (17)

PURPOSE: To give children practice in recognizing words silently.

ACTIVITY: Game.

PROCEDURE: Children may be at their seats or in a circle: Words are held up and all children read silently, performing an action. Example: CAR–turn steering wheel; GO FAST–SLOW–STOP–EAT–WALK–SLEEP–SPEED LIMIT 10 MPH–AIRPLANE–READ–SING–UPSTAIRS.

MATERIALS: Have a variety of cards about 4 x 6 inches, with a variety of action words on the cards pertaining to a trip.

TITLE: FISHING   (18)

PURPOSE: This is a game to motivate children to learn new words and review old ones; also, it provides practice in constructing meaningful sentences.

ACTIVITY: Game.

PROCEDURE: A child in his reading group goes fishing in a "pond" for a "fish" (a fish-shaped card with a word from their reader printed on one side). There are several "fish" in the "pond." When he "catches" a fish, he must try to pronounce that word correctly; then he chooses another child to go fishing. When all the fish are caught and laid on the pier (a table or chalk tray), the children try to construct a meaningful sentence from them. The words on the card will be such that this is possible. A magnet tied by a string to a stick makes a pole. Each fish should have a couple of paper clips pinned to it so they may be picked up by the magnet.

ILLUSTRATION:

TITLE: WORD REVIEW GAME   (19)

PURPOSE: To provide motivation for word review.

ACTIVITY: Game.

PROCEDURE: On a ditto master, draw pictures of rocket ships with words printed on them. The children who need to learn these words are allowed to color a rocket when they know the word written on it. The one who gets his rockets colored first will be the first one to land on the moon.

ILLUSTRATION:

TITLE: PAIRS-PEARS   (20)

PURPOSE: To have children learn that some words sound alike but look different and have different meanings (homonyms).

ACTIVITY: Game.

MATERIALS: Heavy paper and a felt pen for marking a set of cards (you make) with homonyms.

DIRECTIONS: Two to six players. Cards are shuffled and dealt out in rows, face down. The first player turns over two cards—if they "match," the player keeps them and has another turn. If not, he turns them face down and the next player tries to match two cards. The player with the most pairs (pears) wins the game.

ILLUSTRATION:

HERD	BARE	WOULD	ROWS
SO	Sew	WRITE	SEE
BEAR	HEIR	WOOD	DEER
RIGHT	DEAR	ROSE	BORE
AIR	HEARD	SEA	BOAR

TITLE: SPIN-A-WORD   (21)

PURPOSE: To aid in word recognition, review, and meaning.

ACTIVITY: Game.

PROCEDURE: Eight words are written on a disc. In the center of the disc is a spinner. This spinner is movable. The class divides into teams. Each child from a team spins the spinner. The word the spinner lands on must be pronounced, spelled, and defined. If the child misses, the next team gets a chance to say the word correctly. The child who misses *remains* in the group. The children who say the word correctly return to their seats.

ILLUSTRATION:

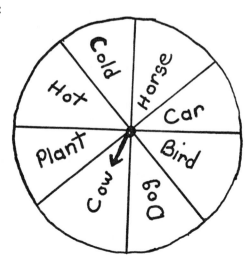

TITLE: JET GAME (22)

PURPOSE: Sight vocabulary drill.

ACTIVITY: Game.

PROCEDURE: The children are divided into two groups, each child representing a leader of the jet squadron. The word cards are flashed to the first jet (first child) of each squadron and then to the rest of the jets in order. Any child who does not know the word card which is flashed to him is given the card. The jets are not ready to go if any child in the squadron has a word card. Which squadron will be able to take off first?

TITLE: WORD BUILDING–ADD-A-LETTER (23)

PURPOSE: To develop vocabulary by adding initial letters to phonograms.

ACTIVITY: Game.

PROCEDURE: Divide the class into groups of no more than eight. Give each group one card with a common ending, such as:

Each group places a stack of cards on their table. Each card has the letter of the alphabet on it. There is only one card for each letter of the alphabet. Each student will draw one card from the stack and then try to match it to the group's word-ending card. If the letter will make a whole word, the student who drew the card writes the new word down on his list. If he cannot make a new word, he "discards" the letter. When all the letters are gone, the game is over. The player with the most words on his list wins. After each group has finished a game, they may trade word-ending cards.

Blends, digraphs, and diphthongs may also be used instead of, or in combination with, the single letters of the alphabet.

TITLE: CARD GAME   (24)

PURPOSE: To learn homonyms.

ACTIVITY: Game.

PROCEDURE: Many children have a hard time understanding homonyms. These words are often confusing to the child and should be practiced whenever possible. A card game could be made up in which the object of the game would be to make as many pairs as possible. Two or more children could play, depending on how many pairs of words were made up in the deck.

This game is similar to the game Fish, which most children already know how to play. Seven cards are dealt to each player. Player #1 asks Player #2 if he has a certain word. If Player #2 has this "word," he must give it up. If he does not have it, Player #1 must go fishing in the remainder of the deck. The game is played until the deck runs out. The player with the greatest amount of pairs wins.

TITLE: SPINNING FOR ANTONYMS   (25)

PURPOSE: To review antonyms.

ACTIVITY: Game.

PROCEDURE: Construct a wheel out of paper. Put an arrow on the wheel that will spin around. Divide the wheel into sections and write a word in each section. Divide the class into two teams. Select a person to spin the arrow and a person to keep score. Have one child from each team go to the blackboard. Then the spinner spins the arrow. As soon as the arrow stops on a word, the two children at the board turn and write the antonym of the word the arrow stopped on. The first child to finish writing the correct word is the winner and wins a point for his team. The game continues until each player has had a turn. Then the points are tallied and the winning team declared.

ILLUSTRATION:

TITLE: FIND THE MISSING WORD (26)

PURPOSE: Word recall.

ACTIVITY: Game.

PROCEDURE: A list of not more than six spelling words are written on the board (this list would be lower if the grade level was below grade 2). The children would be asked to look at the words. An approximate time limit should be given at this point for viewing the words. The class should be divided into two (2) teams. One person from each team goes to the back of the room where he cannot see the board. When these two children leave, one of the words is erased. The children return, and the first child to recognize the missing word gains a point for his team. If this is used for the intermediate grades, several words could be erased at a time.

ILLUSTRATION:

Board #1

Bat
Cow
Bird
Horse
Lamb
Dog

Board #2

Bat
Cow
Bird
Horse
- - - -
Dog

children
hiding

TITLE: FOOTBALL (27)

PURPOSE: The purpose of this game is to increase vocabulary power by using words in sentences.

ACTIVITY: Game.

MATERIALS: Materials needed are a list of words of common difficulty or currently being stressed, a chalkboard, and chalk.

PROCEDURE: The team to make the first play is the one whose captain wins the toss of the coin. The teacher or pupil leader pronounces a word, and the first player on Team I uses it in a sentence. If correct, his football, which is drawn on the 0-yard line on the chalkboard, moves to the 10-yard line. The first player on Team II is then given a word to use in a sentence and if he does so correctly, his ball moves to the

10-yard line from its end of the field. The team to cross the opponent's goal line first is declared the winner.

The following words will be used in today's game: population, feast, century, parents, dimly, country, bias, prejudice, Caucasian, ache, nameless, tiring, taxes, through, thoughtfulness, tirelessly, trained, wayside, and woke.

A simulated football field is drawn on the chalkboard before the toss of the coin. If time is limited, then the football field can be drawn on a piece of cardboard or wrapping paper similar to the illustration below. Also regular dimestore footballs can be used, with teams' names being placed on each. When the teacher has the time, the game can be played and finished on another day or at another hour.

ILLUSTRATION:

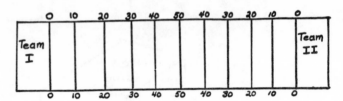

TITLE: DOES IT RHYME? (28)

PURPOSE: As a follow-up for reading groups, this game will reinforce the learning of word meanings which have been introduced in a reading lesson.

ACTIVITY: Game.

PROCEDURE: On large cardboard cards, print the reading words introduced for that day. On smaller cards, write words that rhyme with them. Place the large cards in the chalk tray so the group can see them. Give each student five of the smaller cards. When a student finds a card he thinks will rhyme with the reading word, he takes it to the board to check similarities or compares the two from his seat. He then pronounces the compared words for the teacher, who marks a point for his team if his verbal comparisons match.

ILLUSTRATION:

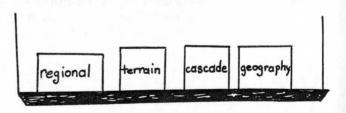

TITLE: REMEMBERING (SYNONYM)   (29)

PURPOSE: To help children remember synonyms.

ACTIVITY: Game.

PROCEDURE: This game is similar to the TV game Concentration. It can be constructed by taking a sheet of poster board, cardboard, or plywood and drawing lines on it so as to divide it into an even number of measured squares. (30 would be an average number.) The squares are numbered from 1 to however many squares there are. In each individual square, a "pocket" (made from construction paper, for example) is attached to the board. A card with a matching synonym written on it is placed in each pocket, the back facing out.

The class is then divided into two groups, Team 1 and Team 2. A child from either group begins the game by choosing one of the numbered squares. The card in the pocket of that square is turned around so the class can see the word. The student then chooses another numbered square. If the two cards match (have the identical words), then that team gets another chance and will continue until the cards are mismatched. Those that are matched stay "face to" in their pockets. If the team mismatched the cards, they are turned "back to" in their pockets and the opposing team gets the turn. The game continues until all the cards have been turned "face to."

This is an educational and enjoyable game that may help the children with reading, and with training them to retain things they are taught.

4 Bolstering Phonic Skills to Decipher Words in Group Activities

• • • • • • • • • • • • •

Isn't phonics a bore? Can anyone get enthused about macrons and breves, the long and short of it? We must face it—blends, digraphs, and diphthongs too do not appeal to students, but they are important for students to learn as a means of acquiring phonic skills.

In this chapter, you will find interesting phonic lessons to supplement whatever reading material you are using. These ideas are designed to help you attract the attention of your students and sustain their interest. To help you maintain flexibility, contained in this chapter are group activities useful for introducing a phonic element or for reinforcing a previous learning.

If you are an intermediate grade teacher, you undoubtedly have some students who are lacking in phonic knowledge. These activities will be useful to you because you can group students for a particular skill need and use the ideas presented.

Teachers at all levels will find these energizers useful in meeting the phonic needs of their students, and besides being useful, they will be interesting to your students and add a new dimension to your teaching performance.

TITLE:	INTRODUCTION OF CONSONANTS AND BLENDS	(1)

PURPOSE: To teach consonants and blends.

ACTIVITY: Group.

PROCEDURE: To introduce the sounds of consonants and blends, give each child a sheet of paper with pictures of objects. Direct the class to circle the objects that have the sounds you have put on the board. Each sound will be represented by a different-colored crayon circle.

Put this on the board:

sh—red crayon
wh—green crayon
th—blue crayon
ch—yellow crayon

ILLUSTRATION:

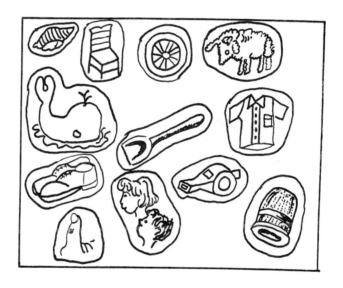

TITLE: CONSONANT TEAM—(th)   (2)

PURPOSE: To teach the consonant digraph, th.

ACTIVITY: Group.

PROCEDURE: On a bulletin board or poster board, make the body of a turkey (without feathers). For practice with the *th*-consonant digraph team, ask the children to think of words starting with the *th* sound that have the same sound. Have at least ten words written up on pieces of paper or poster board. Also have lots of feathers cut out, which they can

81

paper-clip together with the words and then tack or paper-clip to the body of the turkey.

Words used in this activity can be: three, thank, thanks, think, thumb, thimble, thirteen, throne, thread, thorn, thermos, and others.

ILLUSTRATION:

TITLE: CONSONANT TEAM–(sh)   (3)

PURPOSE: To learn the *sh*-consonant digraph.

ACTIVITY: Group.

PROCEDURE: For practice with the consonant team–*sh*, make the body (a simple circle with eyes and funny mouth) of an octopus. Have the children name some words with *sh* beginning each word and sounding the same. As the child names a word or words, have the words written on cards which can be paper-clipped to the tentacles of the octopus. The octopus can have many tentacles with many words.

The same thing can be done with the consonant team—*ch*, but make a chicken out of construction paper or cardboard and staple it to a poster or bulletin board. The children can then find words beginning with that consonant team which sound the same. The words can be paper-clipped to "eggs." The children can fill the hen's nest with such words.

Words that can be used are, shark, ship, shelf, share, shirt, shoe, sheep, shovel, shave, and shell. For the *ch*, such words as church, chalk, children, chair, chop, chain, chimney, checker, and cherry can be utilized.

ILLUSTRATION:

TITLE: VOWEL SOUNDS   (4)

PURPOSE: This game helps the children learn their vowel sounds.

ACTIVITY. Group.

PROCEDURE: The teacher pastes pictures on cards and writes the words underneath the picture (the vowel letters are omitted). The children then write the words on their papers, adding the vowel letters as they write.

ILLUSTRATION:

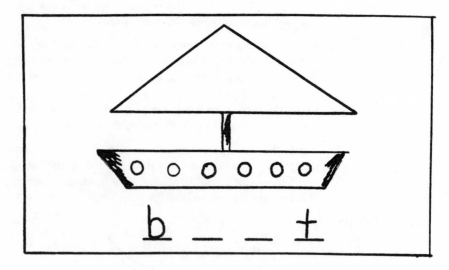

TITLE: RHYMING STORY (5)

PURPOSE: To aid comprehension and spelling of words which rhyme.

ACTIVITY: Group.

MATERIALS: The week's spelling words.

PROCEDURE: Write one of the spelling words on the board and tell the children to make up a story using as many rhyming words as possible. *Example:* cake, rake, sake, make, lake, bake, fake, take, wake.

TITLE: "I'M THINKING" GAME (6)

PURPOSE: Auditory and visual review of phonetic elements.

ACTIVITY: Group.

PROCEDURE: Write several vocabulary words on the board or on poster board, such as the following:

> price
> April
> plow

Have the children find and read words in response to leads such as these, which may be given by the teacher or various pupils.

"I see a word with a soft *c* in it." (price)

Note: Several words could be correct for one question.

"I'm thinking of a word that has a consonant blend in the middle." (April)

"I'm thinking of a word that has *o-w* in it as in *cow*." (plow)

TITLE: SOUND IDENTIFICATION STORY   (7)

PURPOSE: Recognition of beginning sounds.

ACTIVITY: Group.

PROCEDURE: Make up a list of the letters that the group is having the most trouble identifying by sound. Write a story, using as many words as possible which begin with these letters. Pass out cards to the children so that each child has one card with a letter on it. Read the story and each child will hold up his card as he hears a word that begins with the letter he is holding. This is also good for listening skills.

TITLE: WHO AM I?   (8)

PURPOSE: To develop initial letter sounds.

ACTIVITY: Group.

PROCEDURE: Teacher says "I am thinking of someone in this room whose name starts the same as dog, donkey, and diaper. Who can it be?" When a child realizes that his name begins with the same sound, he joins the teacher in front of the class, or he goes to the back of the room or perhaps to the library table. If there are others in the class who do not catch on as quickly, you may say the words again or give three different words. The children may stay up with the teacher or go back to their seats while the teacher gives another set of words with a different letter.

TITLE: AUDITORY PERCEPTION OF BLENDS   (9)

PURPOSE: To reinforce the auditory perception of blends.

ACTIVITY: Group.

PROCEDURE: Assign each child in the reading group a beginning consonant blend. A story would be told having words containing the blends. As the story is told, each child is to listen for his word blend. As soon as he hears the words, he is to raise his hand. For each word he hears, he gets 1 point. The first child to get 10 points is the winner.

TITLE:	SENTENCE RELAY (10)
PURPOSE:	Phonics practice.
ACTIVITY:	Group.
PROCEDURE:	Form from two to four teams. Have the first player on each team go to the board and write a word. Each member of the team in succession adds a word to the sentence, but each new word must begin with the last letter of the preceding word. The team that completes an intelligent sentence using all its players wins the game.
EXAMPLE:	The elves saw wonderful lakes.

TITLE:	"HEAR YE" BLENDS (DIGRAPHS OR DIPHTHONGS) (11)
PURPOSE:	Auditory discrimination—*sounds*.
ACTIVITY:	Group.
PROCEDURE:	Distribute one card to students, on which a word is written and the first two letters (blends, digraphs, or diphthongs) are underlined.

One at a time, the students stand up and say only the beginning sound of their word. Classmates will have five chances to try to guess the word on the student's card. If a student guesses the correct word, he may replace the first student. If no one guesses the word after five tries, the student is given a point for his team.

ILLUSTRATION:

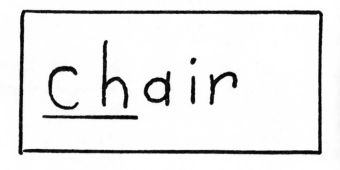

TITLE: COLOR-OBJECT GAME   (12)

PURPOSE: To help distinguish between rhyming words with the same beginning sounds.

ACTIVITY: Group.

PROCEDURE: Combine a lesson in color with a study of beginning sounds, by pairing objects to colors that start with the same letter.

Example:		
Blue boat	Crimson car	
Red rope	Brown bat	
Yellow yo-yo	Purple pencil	
Green gate	White whale	

TITLE: PUPPET VOWELS   (13)

PURPOSE: To teach the long and short sound of the vowels.

ACTIVITY: Group.

MATERIALS: Chart, bag puppets, word cards [See Chapter 8, activity (20) for making puppets.]

PROCEDURE: The children can have so much fun with hand puppets. They are excellent for speech development activities in reading class. These puppets have the label of the long and short vowel sound placed on each puppet. As there are five vowels and the long and short sound for each, you will be able to have ten children participating at one time. The other children will enjoy watching too.

Introduce the vowel sounds by discussing the chart. Then the teacher may read a story, and, as she comes to a word that she wants to attack phonetically (discovering whether the vowel is long or short), she holds up the word card and the child steps forward and manipulates his puppet as he says the word. As there will be two children with the same vowel, they will have to be sure that the sound is either long or short before either one steps forward. The class will enjoy using the puppets in a story, in sentences, or just using word cards. If the teacher would like, she could have a group do this as independent study skills. It would give the children good practice. One child could hold the cards while the other children played with the puppets. The cards would have to have the long or short symbol on the back to help the child who was displaying the cards.

ILLUSTRATION:

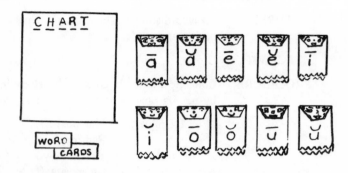

TITLE: LETTER SOUNDS (14)

PURPOSE: To learn letter sounds.

ACTIVITY: Group.

PROCEDURE: In the first grade, transparencies can be utilized in the reading period. Besides being educational and a very good teaching aid, they are colorful and keep the attention of the child. A wise teacher will realize this and also use the overlay as an added dimension.

The following pictures start with the *c, ca,* or *ch* sound. Have the class say what each picture is and tell them each picture starts with a *c*.

ILLUSTRATION:

88

TITLE: CONSONANT BLEND GAME   (15)

PURPOSE: To develop consonant blends.

ACTIVITY: Group.

PROCEDURE: Prepare a set of cards with a consonant blend on each one such as *st, sm, sp, sk,* etc. Divide the class into two teams, and in turn each one will draw a card. If a child recognizes the blend, he must give an example of a word using it. For example, if the child chose a card with the blend *sm,* he could say a word such as "small" or "smart." Scores should be kept for each team.

ILLUSTRATION:

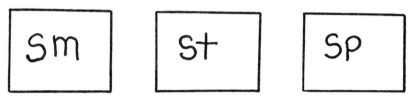

TITLE: READING POETRY ALOUD FOR PHONICS PRACTICE (16)

PURPOSE: To build listening skills.

ACTIVITY: Group.

MATERIALS: A poem.

PROCEDURE: Choose any poem to read aloud. Choose a particular sound to listen for (for example, the long *a* sound). Have the children raise their hands whenever they hear that particular sound in the poem. Many children will raise their hands when they hear sounds that are similar to the sound being listened for, but not actually the same sound. (For instance, they might mistake the word *their* as having the long *a* sound.) This will give you an opportunity to talk about other closely related phonetic sounds and how to distinguish between them.

TITLE: VOWEL HOUSE   (17)

PURPOSE: Reinforce long and short vowel sounds.

ACTIVITY: Group.

PROCEDURE: A house is drawn for each vowel sound. One of them will be a junk house. One child will be the doorkeeper—or if more children could be involved, use one child as a door-keeper for each house. Make up cards with a word which uses one of the vowel sounds.

A child with a card says, "May I sleep in your house to-night?"

The doorkeeper answers, "Yes, you may, if your name is alright. What is your name?"

The child with the card replies "My name is soap."

The doorkeeper puts the child's name or initial on the house.

If wrong, the child must sleep in the junk house.

ILLUSTRATION:

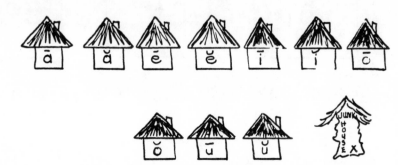

TITLE: PICTURE CARDS   (18)

PURPOSE: Matching pictures of objects or activities with the appropriate word to improve recognition of initial and ending sounds.

ACTIVITY: Group.

PROCEDURE: Paste clippings from magazines, etc. on 3" x 5" index cards. The clippings should represent familiar objects or activities of children. On the reverse side, print the word that names or describes the picture.

Arrange students informally around the teacher. Begin by showing a picture to a child. If he identifies it correctly, ask him for the initial letter sound in the word (or ending sound or spelling). If he answers correctly, give him the card to hold. If he is incorrect, move to the next child and let him try. Proceed in this manner until all cards have been won by the children. The child who holds the most cards wins the game.

ILLUSTRATION:

Card Front   Card Back

TITLE:	SWIM IN THE SEA OF "S" WORDS (19)
PURPOSE:	To help the children recognize the initial consonant sound of *s*.
ACTIVITY:	Group.
MATERIAL:	Poster with slots in which appropriate flash cards can be inserted (see below). Flash cards with appropriate words printed on them.
PROCEDURE:	(1) Have a short discussion on the initial consonant sound of *s*.
	(2) Bring out the poster and insert proper words to help reinforce previous discussion.

ILLUSTRATION:

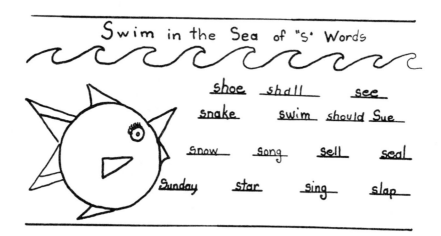

TITLE: OUR BIG BOOK OF BLENDS   (20)

PURPOSE: This motivational device is designed to teach and reinforce blends.

PROCEDURE: The book is constructed of poster board, (yellow front and back, with white pages), held together with three metal ring binders. Each page has hand-drawn colored pictures, two to a page, illustrating each different word containing a blend. Below each picture, the word is printed in black with the front blend missing. A slot with a pocket to hold the proper blend card has been cut out of the page at the front of the printed word. A pile of bright, yellow blend cards with the blend sounds printed in black is placed beside the book. I chose *sh, ch, wh,* and *th* for this mini-lesson, with such words as church, shirt, children, shovel, chimney, shoe, thimble, thumb, shell, cherries, whale, wheel, cheese, whistle, whip, and chicken.

The teacher holds the book and opens it to the first picture, a church. Beneath the picture is printed the letters *urch*. The teacher calls on a child to come and identify the picture. As the child says the word church, he is asked to emphasize the front blend sound in order to determine whether *sh* or *ch* should be placed in front of it to complete the word. He is promptly reinforced both by the teacher's approval and by actually *placing* the *ch* blend card in the slot to complete the word. This process is carried on throughout the book, with different children taking different words.

This book may be used for individual activities as well. It can be placed on the activity table for use when a child has completed his work and wishes something to do, or it may be taken to his desk for a quiet activity of practicing his blend sounds. Two children may use it at the same time, one acting as the teacher, the other the participant, each correcting and reinforcing each other.

As the class learns more sounds and words, the ring binders enable extra pages to be added. The possibilities are unlimited for the addition of more words and the inclusion of blend sounds that may occur other than at the beginning of a word.

ILLUSTRATION:

TITLE:	GROCERY SHOPPING (21)
PURPOSE:	To provide practice in listening for beginning consonant sounds.
ACTIVITY:	Group.
MATERIALS:	Fifty or more items which can be bought at the grocery written on index cards; a large bag; teacher's list of words with all the key consonant sounds.
PROCEDURE:	Children pick out three or more cards which are in the large bag.

The teacher says, "Did anyone buy anything with the same first sound as _____?" Whatever the key word is, the children with any cards containing items which begin with that sound go put their item on the shelf (could be the chalk tray).

Key Words: Sugar Ham Carrots Syrup
Game Words: Shortening Honey Candy Celery Hominy
  Cottage Cheese Soup

TITLE: MAKE A WORD   (22)

PURPOSE: Improve initial sounds of words and understanding of word blends.

ACTIVITY: Group.

MATERIALS: Large flannel board, felt squares with word endings (i.e., *im, ug, ant, ap, at, end, ag, og, ip, ank, it, asp, ash, ep,* etc.) printed on them, clown hats with two-letter consonant blends (i.e., *sl, fr, dr, cl, tr, pr, pl, sp, sh, gr, ch, st, sm, fl, sn,* etc.) printed on them, and one large clown face.

PROCEDURE: Put clown face on flannel board, then place one of the word endings on his forehead. Place the consonant blend hats down on each side of the flannel board and ask the children to make a word by choosing a hat for the clown. Each new word they make can be written on the chalkboard in order to show them how many ways you can make words by changing the consonant blend. Then change the ending and make some more words. Teams can be used for making words, also.

Note: Imagination can be used in choosing the objects for the flannel board (such as cups and saucers, circles cut in half, wedges from a pie, apples cut in half, eyes on a face, etc.). Word endings (*ing, ed,* etc.) can be introduced with this basic idea also.

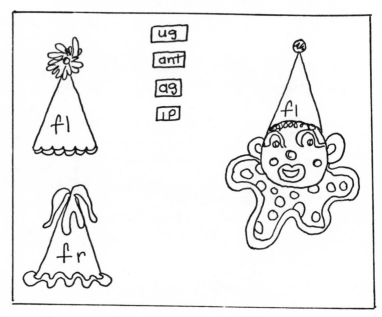

TITLE: RHYMING WORDS   (23)

ACTIVITY: Group.

PROCEDURE: Make a train with many cars out of poster board or thick cardboard. The train can stand up in the chalk tray of the blackboard. Have the children take a car and find in a box of words a card which has two rhyming words, like cat and rat. When a child finds a card with two such words, let him paper-clip the card to the train car and place it behind the engine of the train. The train can be as long as the teacher wants it to be.

In the box containing the cards with two words on them, have some cards which do not rhyme, like cat and eat.

This can also be used with opposite words, blends, or whatever the teacher would like to use that day.

Make the train colorful and the activity fun.

ILLUSTRATION:

TITLE: FINDING CONSONANTS   (24)

PURPOSE: To provide practice in identifying beginning sounds.

ACTIVITY: Group.

MATERIALS: Selected pictures with items whose names begin various consonant sounds.

PROCEDURE: The teacher holds up a picture and asks, "Who can find a picture of something that starts with a D?" The children can either answer orally or write down their answer on paper.

A variation of this can be, "Find as many things in this picture as you can that begin with a D."

TITLE: VOWEL SENTENCES   (25)

PURPOSE: To provide practice in finding vowel sounds.

ACTIVITY: Group.

PROCEDURE: Using the five vowels, the students make up a sentence of five words, using each of the sounds. Example: Have I seen you about?
a i e
o u

You are not in here.
u a o i e

This should be given to advanced children. It is especially good for those who finish work early. It can be made harder by specifying use of only long or only short vowels.

TITLE: LONG OR SHORT VOWELS   (26)

PURPOSE: To teach the children to identify the different vowel sounds.

ACTIVITY: Group.

PROCEDURE: Divide the class into five groups—a, e, i, o, and u. Have them collect pictures from magazines, catalogues, and newspapers which illustrate their vowel. Each group takes turns showing one of their pictures and sounding only the vowel. Then they call on another member of the class to tell whether it is long or short.

TITLE: PHONIC BASEBALL   (27)

PURPOSE: To give students practice in recognizing similarities in beginning sounds.

ACTIVITY: Group game.

PROCEDURE: On a chalkboard, draw a baseball diamond and write a word on each base. To make a home run, a pupil must say a word that has the same initial sound as the word on the base. If a pupil misses, he is out. Later on, when pupils have had more practice, have them choose teams and play the game. Three outs bring the other team to bat.

This game can be changed to provide practice in recognition of similarities in word endings.

5 Gaming Activities for Developing Phonic Abilities

• • • • • • • • • • • • •

You will find 21 phonic games in this chapter to help you motivate your students and individualize your reading program. The blending games, phonogram hunts, vowel discrimination games, and initial sound games will provide you with interesting material which will enrich your teaching strategies and provide highly motivating reinforcement learning material for your students.

These gaming ideas are simple to execute yet productive in achieving results, since students enjoy fun activities. They can carry on these games in small groups with a minimum of your time involved because the intrinsic motivation provided by the games themselves will sustain intense student interest.

Besides being highly motivating, independent games can be trusted aides in providing learning reinforcement of sufficient dosage to help children overlearn phonic skills necessary for accurate word attack. While it is sometimes necessary and desirable to teach to groups, there are other times when students can more profitably work independently because small groups facilitate pupil involvement and permit individualization of instruction to meet specific student needs.

With a little thought and imagination, you can revise some of the ideas presented to fit other phonic learnings. For example, the "Initial Letter and Blend Baseball Game" could be played by using diphthongs and digraphs, too.

Another method of increasing the utility of some of these games is to draw the illustration on a transparency, omitting the words or letters. For example, the "Paper Flowers" game contains a picture of a flower. Put the flower on a transparency the usual way using a photocopying machine, and with grease pencil or felt pen, write the words or letters. Since both grease pencil and felt pen marks are easily eradicated by rubbing the transparency with a moist cloth, the transparency can be used for a variety of things, giving you flexibility and high utility.

When gaming activities are available and appropriate to students' needs, high motivation and learning interest will help carry your students to higher plateaus of reading achievement.

TITLE: ROLL-A-BLEND   (1)

PURPOSE: Learning consonant blends.

PROCEDURE: Using a multi-sided block with consonant blends printed on each surface, the game proceeds with one person casting the block and each of the players building as many words as possible beginning with that blend.

Scoring will be done by the awarding of 1 point per each correct word spelled out and 1 point deducted from the score for each improper word used.

ILLUSTRATION:

TITLE: VOWEL TRAIN RIDE   (2)

PURPOSE: To give students practice discriminating vowel sounds.

MATERIALS: Cardboard "train"—engine and six cars; cards with single words written on them, taken mainly from Dolch's 220-Word List.

PROCEDURE: 1. Pass out five cards to five players.

2. "Today we are going to take a train ride. How many of you would like to go?

"Before we go, we must fill the cars. To do this, we put in words whose vowel sounds are the same as the vowel sound of the name of the picture on each car. Each car will hold three words.

"When it is your turn, come up and go through your cards one by one, saying each word. If you have a card with a word on it that has the same sound as one of the train cars, then put the word on that car, like this (show example).

"If you have a word for which there is no train car, then you must take it to the engineer and tell him the vowel sound so that maybe later he can add some more cars to take care of the extra words."

3. When all children have had their turns at placing their cards, say "Now our train is all loaded and we're ready to go."

TITLE: **VOWELS REINFORCEMENT**   (3)

PURPOSE: Phonics reinforcement.

PROCEDURE: Make large cards (at least 7" by 8") from poster board. On ten of the cards, print the vowels with the long and short markings. On the remaining cards, draw pictures representing familiar words or use sight and reading vocabulary.

Set the vowel cards up against the blackboard with the long vowels on one side and the short ones on the other side. Divide the class into two teams and set up a scorekeeping chart on the board. Hold up one card at a time. If a member of team #1 places it behind the correct vowel card, his team gets a point. If either team catches a mistake of the other team and corrects it, they get the point. High score wins the game.

TITLE: **INITIAL LETTER AND BLEND BASEBALL GAME**   (4)

PURPOSE: To develop skill in using initial letters and to make words.

PROCEDURE: To make a home run, a child is to think of four words, each beginning with a letter from each base, such as *man, like, see, home.*

Variations: Blends can be used for bases, as well as rhyming words.

ILLUSTRATION:

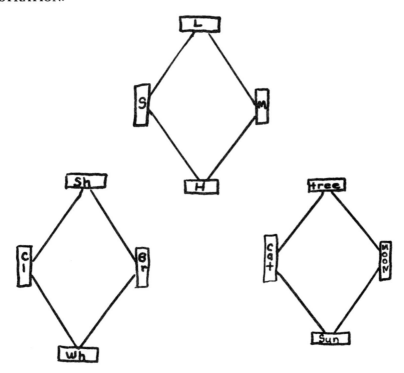

TITLE: SOUND TRAIN   (5)

PURPOSE: This game teaches consonant and blend sounds.

PROCEDURE: Take a row at a time. Once child is the engine and the others are cars of the train. The train is made out of cardboard boxes painted with bright colors. The teacher holds up cards with consonants or consonant blends on them. These are the "signals." When the children see each card, they make the sound that it represents; i.e., *sh* and the children would all say *shhhhhhhhhhh*, until the teacher holds up another signal. A variation of the game is to give each child a card with a letter or a blend on it. One child is the engine. He steams around the room making the sound on his card. At the teacher's signal, he stops. Another child becomes the engine. Both make the engine's sound (the second child's card). Continue for the entire group.

101

TITLE:	PHONOGRAM HUNT (6)
PURPOSE:	The combination of a vowel with one or two consonants is called a phonogram. The main purpose of *Phonogram Hunt* is to develop skill in putting two sounds of three together to build words.
PROCEDURE:	Children who have been conditioned against "reading" and "words" will often learn phonograms rapidly as a game. They can be shown that simply by "hitching" another letter to the front or back of a phonogram, they can build, read, write, and spell words without memorizing them.

ILLUSTRATION:

all	ar	ow	aw

READ THESE WORDS

ball	car	cow	awl
call	far	now	saw
fall	tar	bow	gnaw
tall	mar	how	raw
hall	star	down	paw
wall	barn	owl	shawl

Put these words in rows according to their families, like above:

car	gown	owl	raw
down	paw	tar	now
shawl	mar	ball	hall
call	barn	tall	stall
wall	brown	cow	star
saw	awl	bar	fall
AR	*AW*	*OW*	*ALL*

TITLE: SOUNDS GOOD (7)

PURPOSE: To develop skill in hearing the difference between consonant blends.

MATERIALS: 5" x 8" index cards.

PROCEDURE: The teacher divides her class into two groups or several teams. She shows a card on which is written two consonant blends. To answer correctly, a student must give the sounds of the two consonants and then provide a word for each sound. Example: for blends *CH* and *SH*, use the words *CH*OP and *SH*OP. The teacher selects the student who raises his hand first to give the answer for the card shown.

ILLUSTRATION:

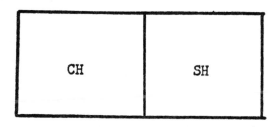

Note: Listing of other consonant blends.

BL, BR, CH, CL, CR, DR, FL, FR, GL, GR,

PL, PR, SC, SCH, SCR, SH, SHR, SL, SM,

SN, SP, ST, STR, SPR, SW, TH, TR, THR, WH, SQU,
SK

TITLE: TREASURE HUNT (8)

PURPOSE: Identifying blends, digraphs, and vowels.
Matching these sounds to words.
Matching words to pictures.

MATERIALS: Box filled with objects or pictures. Word cards corresponding to pictures and objects.

PROCEDURE: Place the box filled with objects or pictures before the children. Have the printed-word cards arranged around the blackboard ledge. Divide the class into teams and let them decide their own team names. When it is each child's turn, have him close his eyes and draw an object or picture from the box. The child must then find the word corresponding to his object or picture and identify the sound or vowel. The winner is the team with the greatest number of correct answers.

TITLE: PICTURE HOUSE (9)

PURPOSE: Phonetic activity for grades 1-3.

MATERIALS: Cut two or more roof peaks along the top of a 9" x 12" sheet of poster board. In each peak, write the letter or letters for the sounds currently being studied. Cut a series of slots in each house. Cut one 2" square of poster board for each slit. On each square, draw a picture containing one of these sounds written on the roofs. Place these picture cards in an envelope and clip to the house.

PROCEDURE: Introduce to the class, "I have a new game. It is called Picture House. On the roof of each house is a letter or combination of letters for a sound we have studied. Below each roof are several slots. In the envelope clipped to the house are picture cards. Put the card in the slot under the correct sound. Do one at a time and continue until you have filled all the slots."

ILLUSTRATION:

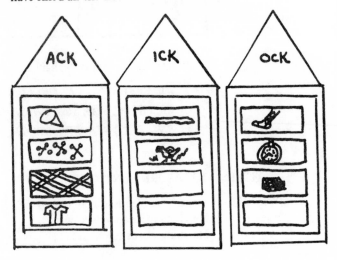

TITLE: VOWEL SOUNDS   (10)

PURPOSE: Phonics reinforcement.

PROCEDURE: Give ten children cards. Each card has a vowel marked either long or short. Have the children form a row in front of the room.

Divide the class into two teams. The teacher gives a word to match up with the correct vowel sound. The vowel card holder will then make the sound of the card he is holding. If the other team does not agree that it is the vowel sound they heard, they get a chance for the point. Each correct one gets a point for their team and the highest score wins.

ILLUSTRATION:

TITLE: SHOPPING AT THE SUPERMARKET   (11)
(Suitable for the First Grade)

PURPOSE: Shopping at the supermarket is a game that a group of first graders can play to give them practice in learning the beginning sounds of words.

MATERIALS: The materials needed are a small shopping bag and picture cards or pictures of items found in the supermarket. The pictures can be cut from magazines, drawn by the teacher, or drawn by the students.

PROCEDURE: The pictures are distributed to each of the children. There is no limit to the number of pictures used. Each child puts his picture cards out on his desk, which becomes a counter with him as the clerk. One child is chosen to be the shopper and takes the shopping bag. He says, "I am going to shop for all things that begin with a *b* sound." He goes from desk to desk, and, as he sees a picture, he says, "Mary, I would like the butter and some bread please." If the shopper doesn't take all cards on the desk beginning with the *b* sound and Mary can catch him, he must give up the shopping bag and then Mary takes over. The game goes on from beginning sound to beginning sound until the shopper makes a mistake.

ILLUSTRATION:

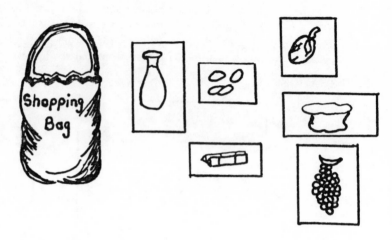

TITLE: MATCHING SOUNDS (12)

PURPOSE: Reinforcement of phonics.

PROCEDURE: Make cards like a regular deck of playing cards. One group should have vowels with a long mark and the other vowels with a short mark. On the rest of the cards, put pictures or words that the children should know or are learning.

The vowel cards are to be placed in two horizontal rows, with the *long a* card above the *short a* card. The other picture or word cards are to be divided equally among the players. One person should have all the cards with the blue edges, one with the green edges, etc. Each player takes a turn saying the word and placing his card (one) under the right vowel sound. At the end of the game, each color can be checked against a master sheet and the right cards gain 1 point for the player. The child with the highest number of correctly placed cards wins the game.

ILLUSTRATION:

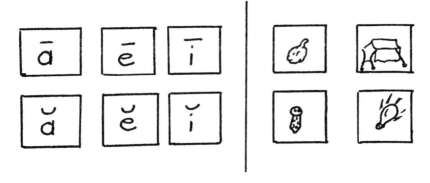

TITLE: PAPER FLOWERS (13)

PURPOSE: To review words that rhyme.

PROCEDURE: Construct several paper flowers. Write a key word in the center of each flower (several different key words should be used). Then write a word on each petal of the flower. Some of the words should rhyme with the key word and some should not. Place the flowers around the classroom. Each child picks a flower from somewhere in the classroom. Then he takes the flower back to his desk and sits down. Next go around the room in an orderly fashion having each child stand up and read his key word and then each of the words on the petals. As he reads each word on the petal, he tells whether or not it rhymes with the key word. If he reads all of the words correctly, then he gets to keep the flower for the rest of the day and tape it to the front of his desk.

This game could be made seasonal. *Example:* A turkey for Thanksgiving with rhyming words written on the feathers. Also, the children could make their own rhyming flower, and, if the flower was correct, the child could put his flower up in the classroom.

ILLUSTRATION:

107

WORD GAME   (14)

PURPOSE: Help to increase the child's ability to recognize vowel sounds.

MATERIALS: Give each child a simulated bingo card consisting of 25 squares, with one word in each square. Each of the words will be typical examples of words with either long or short vowel sounds. The children will also be given covering tabs the size of the squares with $\bar{a}, \breve{a}, \bar{e}, \breve{e}, \bar{i}, \breve{i}, \bar{o}, \breve{o}, \bar{u}, \breve{u}$, printed on them.

PROCEDURE: *Example:* When the teacher calls *long i ($\bar{i}$)* each child with a word on his bingo card having a *long i* will place a tab (the appropriate one) over the word. Only one word is marked each time the teacher calls out a vowel, even though the child might have several words with that vowel sound on his bingo card.

The first child to get a horizontal, vertical, or diagonal row of words covered is the winner. He then calls out "Bingo." Once a child has called out "Bingo," he will read the line of words back to the teacher, pronouncing the vowel sounds properly.

ILLUSTRATION:

$\bar{a}$		ride	hot	seat	boat	top		$\breve{a}$
$\bar{e}$		sat	tape	cut	bate	bit		$\breve{e}$
$\bar{i}$		blue	bat	tap	rode	hope		$\breve{i}$
$\bar{o}$		rod	ate	clue	moon	set		$\breve{o}$
$\bar{u}$		seat	bite	hop	rat	cute		$\breve{u}$

TITLE: SNOOPY'S APPLE ORCHARD   (15)

PURPOSE: The purpose of this game is to provide reinforcement of consonant blends, short and long vowel sounds, and "hard" sounding letters, as a reviewing technique or just for fun.

MATERIALS: Poster board, tempera paints, colored paper.

PROCEDURE: (1)   Take a number of blank cards (number is according to the size of the group) and on each one write a blend, digraph, diphthong, *schwa* sound, or whatever the children are having difficulty with. Put them in a container and mix them around.

(2) On each apple, write a corresponding word that can be matched with the directions on each card.

(3) Divide the children into two groups. Have one child from one group draw a card from the box and find the word on the apples that correctly answers what was on the card. If he gets it right, it goes in the good apple basket. If he is wrong, it goes in the rotten apple basket. After the child has finished, it is the other team's chance. Only one student at a time participates. The team who gets the most apples in the good basket wins the game.

ILLUSTRATION:

TITLE: BEGINNING CONSONANTS (16)

PURPOSE: To give each child in the class a chance to identify a word that begins with the same initial consonant.

PROCEDURE: One child is chosen to be the engineer. He stands in front of the class on a make-believe railroad track and says a word such as *book*. Each pupil is given a chance to pay their fare on the train by saying another word that begins with the same consonant. The engineer may at any time change the beginning consonant. When the train is complete, and all children have been given a chance to ride, the train travels around the room dropping off passengers as they arrive "home." The game can also be played using ending consonants, prefixes, or suffixes.

The train is made by the pupils placing their hands on the shoulders of the passenger in front of them.

Example: Engineer—"book"
First student—"boy"
Second student—"bag"
Third student—"car" (cannot ride)
Engineer—"fish"
Fourth student—"fun," etc.

TITLE: POST-OFFICE GAME   (17)

PURPOSE: To learn long and short vowels.

PROCEDURE: This game can be used with small groups or with the whole class. One idea would be to pass out cards in the morning to the entire class and tell them that whenever they want to mail their cards, they can drop them in the correct mailbox in the classroom. The mailboxes are made out of shoe boxes. Cards are used with one-syllable words. Cards should resemble letters. A stamp in the corner would help indicate that the card is a letter. The way to check and see if the child has made the right choice is to have him insert a little name card in the lower left-hand corner. If he has made a mistake, the card can be put in an envelope marked "RE-TURNED—MAILED IN THE WRONG BOX." This way, the child knows he made a mistake and can have a chance later to mail the card again.

After the child has mailed ten or 15 cards correctly, he can receive in the "mail" an envelope with a star inside. If different-colored stars are used for each series of cards, then the child can record his own progress. Progress could also be recorded on a classroom chart.

Each week a different "postmaster" can be chosen to pass back the "return" envelopes and the envelopes with the stars.

110

TITLE: THE SIGN GAME   (18)

PURPOSE: To teach vowels, blends, and consonants.

PROCEDURE: This game can be used as a total class activity or a small-group activity.

When a certain area of study is taken up—for example, vowel blends—the children cut up construction paper and write on each piece each vowel sound they are to learn: *ay, oi, ee,* and *oy*. When all have been made, the teacher prepares a list of words with these sounds in them. She calls out each word very slowly. With each word, the child raises his sign with the vowel sound he thinks he hears. The teacher checks each answer and then writes the word on the board. The person with the most correct answers wins, or the group with the most correct answers wins.

Since many new words can be added, this game builds vocabulary and aids in listening skills.

TITLE: THE MAGICAL "E"   (19)

PURPOSE: Since many pupils seem not to know the meaning of the word with a final or silent "e," it is an activity to help explain the change that occurs when an "e" is added.

MATERIALS: Cards with a letter of the alphabet printed on them; for the vowels, two cards must be made for the long and short sounds. Also, a card must be made for the special "e."

PROCEDURE: Pass out the cards to the pupils. Tell them that you will pronounce a word but they must be careful with the vowels. For example, say the word "not." "Which letters would come up? Let's bring up our magic 'e.' What word do we have spelled? But there's something wrong here? What is it?" Proceed to have them change the vowel and continue with other words.

ILLUSTRATION:

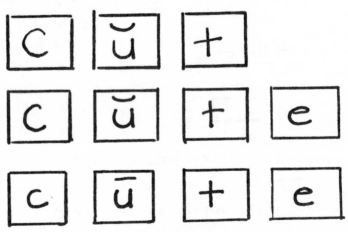

6 Cracking Unknown Words by Structural Analysis

• • • • • • • • • • • • •

As reading teachers, you and I know that producing fully functioning, competent readers is a matter of teaching students a variety of reading skills. Beyond question is the fact that knowledge of structural analysis is a potent skill for decoding unknown words.

Regardless of which reading program you are using for teaching reading, it is likely that none provides sufficient structural analysis lessons for developing this crucial skill among all your students.

In this chapter, you will find games helpful in teaching affixes, compound words, and roots. Group and independent activities are provided to help you supplement the structural analysis dosage given in your reading program. You will be able to choose flexibly among these creative energizers, selecting ideas you deem appropriate for your students' needs. Whether you need a lesson in *ing* words, prefixes, roots, or suffixes, you will find an energizer that is not only usable but tantalizing.

Of all the ideas in this chapter, my favorite is "Prefix Detective." This energizer has utility as an independent or group activity, which is great, but the most interesting thing to me is the way students are intrigued as they puzzle over finding words with the prefixes given. This sleuthing idea is not only fun but also valuable, because it helps students learn to look for affixes as keys to unlocking words.

TITLE: SYLLABLE SLEUTH (1)

PURPOSE: To provide syllabification practice.

ACTIVITY: Group.

PROCEDURE: When teaching the syllables of a new word, let the children clap the beat of the word for variety. For example, in teaching the word *detective*, you would have them say the word in syllables one time and then clap one, two, three,—de-tec-tive, one, two, three, de-tec-tive, or they could stomp their feet to the beat.

This breaks the monotony of trying to explain day after day how the word is divided. Also, clapping to the syllables helps the children remember what to do. Once a child get a "beat" to a word, he will repeat it and come closer to remembering it.

This is a simple method that can be used without elaborate preparations or materials and can be very effective.

ILLUSTRATION:

De-tec-tive
CLAP! CLAP! CLAP!

but-ton

one-two-three

al'pha-bet

base'ball

TITLE: HANGING SUFFIXES (2)

PURPOSE: To develop understanding of suffixes.

ACTIVITY: Group.

PROCEDURE: Tie a clothesline or string across the front of the room. Have words written on clothes-shaped cards that can take the suffix *ing*. The children can pick the words out of a

115

box, and then if they are correct, they can hang them on the line with a clothespin. Have the box full of many kinds of words.

The words can be: like, sing, green, drive, come, fun, jelly, sick, work, joy, taste, real, visit, behind, often, late, hear, and many others. Let the child hang only those that can correctly take the suffix of *ing*.

ILLUSTRATION:

The word cards can be made out of colored construction paper or cardboard. The words can be changed with paper clips or tape. Make the clothes colorful.

TITLE: *ING* FORMS   (3)

PURPOSE: To provide practice in forming *ing* words.

ACTIVITY: Group.

PROCEDURE: The teacher should describe an action and ask the child to say the *ing* word that goes with it. For example, "John talks to Mary. What is John doing?" The response should be "John is talking." This is very good practice for young children.

Other Examples:
Mary watches television.
Fred cuts the grass.
Bill climbs the pole.
Jane calls her dog.

TITLE: VOWEL SOUNDS IN SYLLABLES   (4)

PURPOSE: Provide practice in hearing syllables in one-, two-, and three-syllable words.
Provide practice in word recognition.

ACTIVITY: Group.

MATERIALS: 2" x 6" cards with words from reading book printed on them.

PROCEDURE: Review the rule concerning the number of syllables related to the number of vowels. Get the children to tell the rule if possible. Then select a scorekeeper and pass the box containing the word cards to the first person in Row 1. The child takes a card, says the word, and tells the number of syllables. He is given 2 points if correct and no points if incorrect. Continue until all have had a turn, then add the scores and determine which row had the most correct words as to the number of syllables.

After the game is finished, if the children did not do well, review to help establish in their minds the method of dividing words into syllables. A practice sheet of words could be provided the next day for the children to use in dividing the words written on the paper.

Words to Be Used in This Lesson:

napkin-2	hornet-2	maintain-2	tomato-3
history-3	cucumber-3	permit-2	compare-2
veto-2	allow-2	appoint-2	coal-1
inspect-2	confuse-2	follow-2	huge-1
cannon-2	engine-2	danger-2	alone-2
vacation-3	number-2	number-2	music-2
plaster-2	accident-3	blanket-2	teeth-1
wonder-2	mountain-2	member-2	local-2
problem-2	village-2	danger-2	commit-2
sentence-2	remember-3	surprise-2	proper-2
captain-2	whisper-2	furnace-2	odor-2

TITLE: SYLLABLE FOOTBALL (5)

PURPOSE: To provide practice in dividing words into syllables and in determining the accented syllable.

ACTIVITY: Group.

MATERIALS: Spelling list (two or more syllables).
Large index cards.
Scoreboard (can be drawn on the board).
On the front of the cards are printed the spelling words.
On the back, they are divided into syllables with the accented syllable designated.

PROCEDURE: 1. The class is divided into two teams and are on opposite sides of the room.
2. "Kickoff" is determined by a flip of the coin or picking a number.
3. The first person on the team which won the toss is shown the front of a card. If he can correctly divide the word into syllables, the team gets a "touchdown" worth 6 points.

4. The same person must identify the accented syllable for the extra point. If he cannot identify it, the other team has a chance to try it. If they identify it, they get the point. If they don't, the cardholder gives the answer and the point is lost.
5. After one team has attempted or made the touchdown, it is the other team's turn.
6. Proceed in this manner until the word cards have all been shown. The team with the highest score wins.

ILLUSTRATION: *CARDS*

front	back	scoreboard	
COLONY	COL-O-NY	BOYS	GIRLS

TITLE: INDIAN ACCENT DRILL   (6)

PURPOSE: Stress accented and unaccented syllables.

ACTIVITY: Group.

PROCEDURE: Have the children decorate a coffee can or an old oatmeal box to be used for an Indian drum. Beat out accented and unaccented syllables on the drums.

ILLUSTRATION:

TITLE: SYLLABICATION GAME   (7)

PURPOSE: The purpose is to facilitate the understanding that a syllable contains a vowel sound and makes up a pronounceable unit

118

of a word. Another purpose is to have students learn that some words divide into syllables between double consonants or between two consonants.

ACTIVITY: Game.

PROCEDURE: Divide the reading group into two groups and have them compete by forming words from given syllables. Variations could include matching antonyms, synonyms, building sentences, etc.

ILLUSTRATION:

TITLE: PREFIX DETECTIVE (8)

PURPOSE: To have students learn that many words have prefixes and knowledge of prefixes can help them decode words.

ACTIVITY: Independent.

PROCEDURE: By moving from one square to another (up and down, sidewise or crosswise), see how many words you can find beginning with the prefix *a* and *dis*.

ILLUSTRATION:

D	D	D	O	A	D	A	Z	Z	L	E	P	A
D	I	S	D	D	I	S	U	N	I	T	E	F
A	S	S	T	E	S	O	A	F	I	R	E	O
B	L	I	T	E	C	E	B	O	A	R	D	O
C	I	E	F	U	A	K	O	O	B	I	E	T
F	K	N	A	T	R	A	U	B	U	R	N	L
N	A	P	E	K	D	B	N	D	F	E	E	Y
A	B	A	C	K	B	U	D	I	T	A	D	E
S	L	B	A	L	L	I	I	S	R	S	I	I
I	E	A	B	O	I	L	S	F	A	E	S	D
D	I	S	B	A	N	D	C	A	P	C	O	R
I	T	H	E	A	D	I	O	V	A	D	R	I
S	H	E	N	S	O	N	U	O	D	S	D	O
F	E	D	E	S	I	G	N	R	O	P	E	S
D	I	S	M	O	U	N	T	P	G	F	I	R

TITLE: CHANGING PATTERNS (9)

PURPOSE: To teach word analysis.

ACTIVITY: Group.

PROCEDURE: Present a word to the class that can be enlarged by adding other letters or by changing some letter within the word to make a new word. Have someone in the class identify the word and use it in a sentence. Then change the word and have someone else identify that word and use it in a sentence. Proceed until the class is sure of what is being done and then let the students change the word themselves.

Examples of identifying the word:

Use it in a sentence.
Add an f to the beginning of the word. (fat)
Fat—identify the word.
Use it in a sentence.
Change the t to 11. (fall)
Fall—identify the word.
Use it in a sentence.

Change the a to i. (fill)
Fill—identify the word.
Use it in a sentence.
Change the i to e. (fell)
Fell—identify the word.
Use it in a sentence.

Other good words are ate, ice, end, other, etc.

TITLE:	ANGLING FOR CONTRACTION (10)
PURPOSE:	To reinforce recognition of contractions and their uncontracted forms.
ACTIVITY:	Game.
MATERIALS:	Fifty 3" x 5" index cards. Print contractions on 24 of them and their uncontracted forms on another 24; on remaining two cards, print "Go Fish"; back cards with contact paper and seal front with laminate plastic.
PROCEDURE:	1. Shuffle the cards.
	2. Deal out six cards to each of the five players.
	3. Put the remaining cards in the center.
	4. Each person in turn asks a specific person for a particular card (one that will match a card he holds in his hand). Example: won't, will not.
	5. If the person asked has the card, he must give it up. If he does not have it, he says "Go Fish," and the player draws a card from the pile.
	6. Each time a player gets a pair, he lays the two cards down face up for the others to check.
	7. The first person to discard all cards is the winner.

TITLE:	BATS–BALLS–GLOVES (11)
PURPOSE:	To develop the ability to use a root word and add a prefix or suffix to the root to make a new word.
ACTIVITY:	Independent or small group.
PROCEDURE:	Students will match as many bats (prefixes), balls (root words), and gloves (suffixes) as they can to build new words. This can be used for an individual or in small groups of children—the child with the most new words wins. On each of the bats is a prefix, on each of the balls a root word, and on each of the gloves a suffix.

ILLUSTRATION:

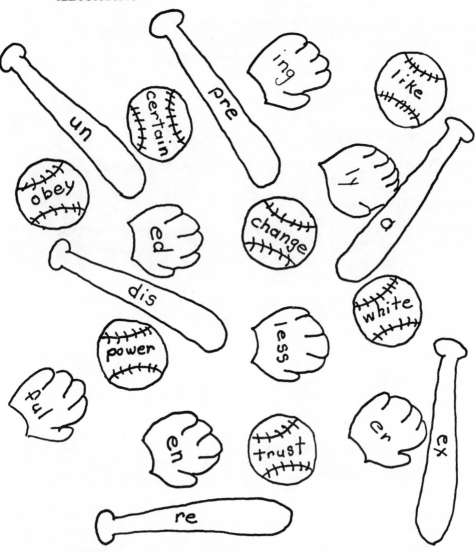

TITLE: FLOWER ROOTS (12)

PURPOSE: To help children gain facility in recognition of form and meaning of a root with a larger word, let them "word flowers." Color the flower around the word.

ACTIVITY: Independent.

MATERIALS: Paper, pencil, words for flowers.

PROCEDURE: Karl's mother had a beautiful garden of lovely flowers. Can you make a pretty garden, too? In each box, a root has been planted. Below is a list of some words that grow from these roots. Put these words on the plants to which they belong. One is done for you. See if you can find more words that come from these roots. Make a flower. Choose any five words you have made. Use each one in a sentence. Be sure your sentence shows that you know the meaning of the word.

ILLUSTRATION: *Words for Flowers*

certainly	happily	encourage	unhappy
discouraged	certainly	uncertain	happiest

TITLE: MAILBOX   (13)

PURPOSE: The mailbox can be used for sorting words that have different endings, for rhyming words, and for words that have the same beginning consonants.

ACTIVITY: Group.

PROCEDURE: Build a simple mailbox out of a heavy piece of cardboard with a frame around it. Cut openings large enough for flash cards to slip through. Add boxes to the back of the frame for the cards to fall into. The procedure for the mailbox is for students to deliver the cards to the right mailbox.

ILLUSTRATION:

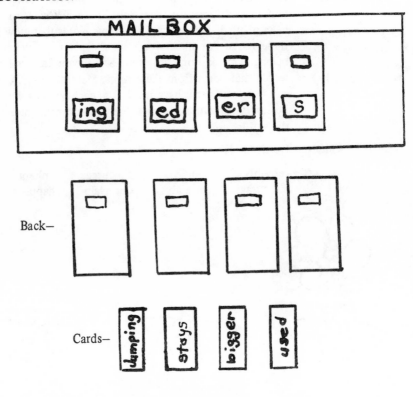

MAIL BOX

Back—

Cards—

TITLE: COMPOUND WORD REVIEW (14)

PURPOSE: To teach compound words.

ACTIVITY: Group.

MATERIALS: Felt board, word cards.

PROCEDURE: "We have been using compound words in our reading, and today we are going to review these words. When we are through with our review, we are going to play a little game using some of them. Can anyone tell me what a compound word is?" ("A word made up of smaller words.")

"Good. Can anyone think of a word that can be found in a compound word?" ("In, some, any, etc..")

"Yes, good. Can you think of anymore?"

("Post, bed, etc.")

"Now I am placing some words on the flannel board, and I want you to see if there are some words we can put together to make a compound word." And so on . . .

Three-Minute Race

The class is divided into several teams, with one person on

124

each team being named "leader." "Using the words, 'some,' 'any,' 'post,' and 'man,' list as many compound words as you can think of. Start when I say 'go' and put pencils down when I say 'stop.' You have three minutes—go!"

ILLUSTRATION:

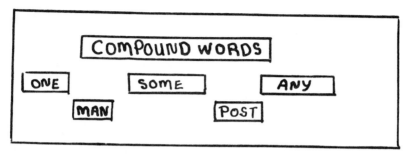

TITLE: BUTTERFLIES GAME (15)

PURPOSE: Butterflies used for forming compound words, prefixes, and suffixes.

ACTIVITY: Game.

PROCEDURE: A bulletin board or a large piece of poster board will supply the background. The teacher goes down the rows assigning a number to each child. She has a spinner with all the numbers represented and spins to determine who will take a turn.

Half of the butterfly will be placed on the poster, the other half of each displayed on the chalk ledge. If the child can create a word out of any of the two halves, making a whole butterfly, he may take the half from the ledge and the other half from the poster.

The winner then is the child with the most butterflies after all have been removed.

This lesson is a game that serves to motivate primary children in the development of word and phonic skills.

ILLUSTRATION:

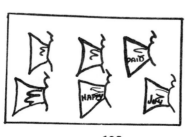

TITLE: AFFIXES BASKETBALL   (16)

PURPOSE: To provide practice in adding suffixes and prefixes.

ACTIVITY: Group.

MATERIALS: Cards with root words on them.
A scoreboard.

PROCEDURE: The class is divided into two teams, prefix and suffix. The teacher shows the first member of the prefix team a root word. He must be able to add a prefix to get a point. Then the suffix team must add a suffix to get a point. The team with the most points wins.

TITLE: OVERHEAD PROJECTOR EXERCISE   (17)

PURPOSE: To familiarize the students with the rule for adding a suffix to a word ending with an *e*. This exercise is for sixth-grade skill building exercises.

PROCEDURE: Prepare with the rule stated on the top and leave a working space below.

RULE: Drop the final *e* before a suffix beginning with a vowel.

Retain the final *e* before a suffix beginning with a consonant.

slot

(line)   _____   _____

Transparent slip with suffixes (more can be added, depending on the words chosen for examples).

ing
tion
ei (i)
ly
ment
sion
less
ness
ty
ful
ly

Example: On the line, in grease pencil, write *confine*. Pull the strip first to *ing* and discuss what to do with the *e*, then pull to *ment* and discuss. Write another word and use two endings, one starting with a vowel and one with a consonant. Discuss each in turn. Do this with a variety of words ending in *e* coupled with the different endings.

TITLE: TREE ROOTS   (18)

PURPOSE: To teach the student that he can spell many words by simply adding prefixes and suffixes to one root word.

ACTIVITY: Group.

MATERIALS: Sketch of a tree on the blackboard.

PROCEDURE: Draw a tree on the board and be sure to sketch in its roots. Choose a simple word like *pay*. Write the word *pay* near a large root on the tree. Discuss the function of a root to a tree, emphasizing that it is basic to all parts of it. Point to the trunk and then the branches of your picture. Ask someone to tell you a word that comes from the root word *pay*. If no one knows one, suggest that by adding a prefix or suffix, they can form a new word from *pay*. Wait until you have most of the possible words from the pupils themselves before adding words yourself. Write each word near a picture of a branch, using colored chalk to distinguish between prefixes and suffixes. When you run out of branches, write the rest of the words created from *pay* in a list. You will have made your point.

TITLE: PRE-ROOT-SUF   (19)

PURPOSE: Children can learn prefixes and suffixes while having fun playing cards.

PROCEDURE: Cut up cardboard to make cards. Then write prefixes, suffixes, or root words on them. Let the children play with them until they are familiar with them. Introduce them to the idea of root words, suffixes, etc. Then let them use the cards to see how many words they can make up, using combinations of root words, prefixes, and suffixes. For example:

pre	school	paid	ed
sub	way	marine	ing
dis	appear	agree	ly
un	cook	fair	d

You can use this same idea to make a card game for the students to play. Make up 52 cards with suffixes, prefixes, and root words. Points are scored according to how many words they form using the different cards. For example, 2 points could be scored for using a prefix and a root word or a root word and a suffix. Five points could be scored for using a prefix, root word, and suffix. Points could even be scored by opponents playing their cards of prefixes and suffixes with someone else's cards. An example would be: A student lays down the "book" *dis-appear*. One of his opponents lays down a card with the prefix *re* on top of his opponent's prefix and scores a point. Later on, the students will have to tell what the prefixes and suffixes mean before they lay their "book" down. Possibilities could go on and on.

TITLE: CATS ON A FENCE   (20)

PURPOSE: To show children how words can be divided into root words, prefixes, and suffixes.

PROCEDURE: On your bulletin board, paint, draw, or attach in some manner a picket fence with black cats sitting on it. Write several words that have either a prefix or a suffix on the picket fence (one word under each cat). Then in white lettering write the root word on the cat's body, the prefix on the cat's head, and the suffix on the cat's tail.

ILLUSTRATION:

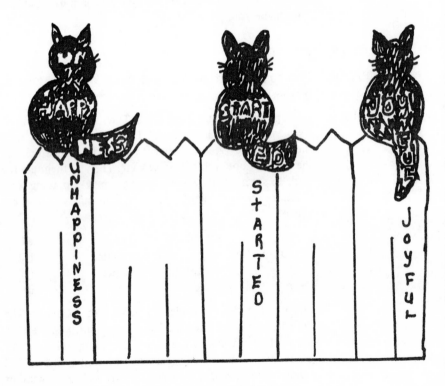

7 Sleuthing for Meaning Using Detective Skills

•   •   •   •   •   •   •   •   •   •   •   •   •

In this chapter, you will find creative ideas for teaching context clues, dictionary skills, and skimming. The relationship among these three activities is hunting. The use of context clues requires searching about in a sentence for clues to the meaning of an unknown word. When using dictionary skills, the reader hunts in his dictionary. By using a skimming technique, the reader scans for specific facts. All are useful skills for fully functioning readers and need reinforcement at all levels. These ideas should help you in providing for development of these skills.

The arrangement of this chapter has the context clue ideas first, followed by dictionary skill activities, and is concluded with a skimming energizer. Each section contains games, group, and independent activities. Some of the group ideas are usable with teams, so you might like to use them as games. Also, some ideas such as puzzles could be used independently as well as in group work.

Group activities are functional with small or large groups. Whenever the whole class needs practice in a particular skill, you can use the idea to teach all of your students. While at times you will have small-group instructions permitting you to meet particular needs, you can use the group ideas and games in this setting, too.

If you will try these ideas, I think you will find that dictionary skill development will become interesting rather than stultifying. Students will respond to these energizers with high interest, making dictionary learning not only less tedious but palatable. When this stage is reached, victory is yours!

TITLE: CLIMB THE LADDER GAME   (1)

PURPOSE: The purpose of this reading game is to help the students develop the skill of defining words with the aid of context clues.

PROCEDURE: Draw two ladders with the same number of rungs on the board. Divide the class into two teams. Ask the first member of one team to tell the meaning of the word after the teacher has read it in the context of a sentence. If he answers correctly, he has climbed one rung up the ladder for his team. Alternate from one member on one team to another member on the other team in asking the meanings for the words. The team that climbs successfully first to the top of their ladder is the winner. This game could be used to review the vocabulary introduced in a unit of reading or for a variety of other skills.

TITLE: DO YOU KNOW THE KEY?   (2)

PURPOSE: To develop skill of using context clues.

ACTIVITY: Group.

MATERIALS: List of sentences containing key words.

PROCEDURE: The teacher dictates sentences containing key words to students, followed by the definition of the key word. Students are told to match the definition with the key word in the sentence. Each sentence contains one key word to be matched with a definition.

> *Example:*   Camels are called "ships of the desert."
> *(Blank)* means "land where the rainfall is scanty."
> (key word is desert)

TITLE: PICTURE CONTEXT CLUE   (3)

PURPOSE: These may be employed to help students use pictures in interpreting new words.

ACTIVITY: Group or independent.

MATERIAL: Magazines, envelopes, scissors.

PROCEDURE: Have children cut pictures from old magazines or workbooks, then make up sentences to go with the pictures. Using as many envelopes as there are pupils, place in each one some stories with matching pictures. Distribute the envelopes. Have each pupil read his story, select a picture that illustrates each, and place it on top of the story it matches.

131

Example: The following story and one of the pictures go together:

She went to see her grandmother. She met a wolf on the way. (Picture of Red Riding Hood)

TITLE: WORD PUZZLE (4)

PURPOSE: To build vocabulary through context clues.

PROCEDURE: Place the correct word from the list at the top of the puzzle into the proper sentence. Clues are taken from the squares as to the number of letters in the word which fits into the sentence.

went	hit
sick	farm
play	tell
red	green
horse	ate

1.
2.
3.
4.
5.
6.
7.
8.
9.
10.

1. Johnny likes to _____ ball after school.
2. The new house is painted _____ .
3. Tim is _____ with a cold.
4. He _____ the little girl with a stick.
5. The old man has pigs on his _____ .
6. Sally has a _____ bicycle.
7. Can you _____ time?
8. We _____ lunch at 12 o'clock.
9. Jerry _____ home after lunch.
10. He rode a big _____ in the parade.

TITLE: NO NONSENSE   (5)

PURPOSE: Sentence meaning/context clues.

ACTIVITY: Group game.

PROCEDURE: On separate pieces of paper or cards, write a different sentence using about three nonsense words. For example,

Team I.   The *zoky shollied* up into the *vax*.

Team II.   When *Raaz* came *kleg*, the baby *chived*.

Each student will be given one sentence which he is to rewrite, replacing the nonsense words with real words that will make the sentence make sense. For example, one student wrote for the above sentences:

The *cat climbed* up into the *tree*.
     1   2   3
When *Daddy* came *home*, the baby *laughed*.
      1   2   3

One student at a time will read his nonsense sentence out loud to the class. He is allowed to choose no more than three classmates, who try to guess which words he chose to replace the nonsense words. For each word they guess correctly, they get 1 point. Each point will be a letter of the word NONSENSE. The first team to spell the whole word wins.

TEAM I   TEAM II

NON _ _ _ _   NON _ _ _ _ _

TITLE: ANIMAL ALPHABET HUNT   (6)

PURPOSE: To give an interesting review in using alphabetical order.

ACTIVITY: Group.

MATERIALS: Duplicated sheets.

PROCEDURE: The teacher passes out duplicated sheets. The children are asked to find the first letter in the alphabet and continue following in alphabetical order until they have completed an animal. The children then identify the animal by filling in the blank provided.

Variation: Chalkboard. Teacher may arrange letters on the chalkboard. Children are asked to find the first letter and the one that comes next. One child then draws a line from A to B. Another child draws a line from B to C. The game continues until the animal is completed and the class has identified it.

133

ILLUSTRATION:

TITLE: ALPHABETIZER   (7)

PURPOSE: To help students learn alphabetical order.

ACTIVITY: Game.

PROCEDURE: This game utilizes a dice cup and five cubes of wood or plastic. A letter of the alphabet is printed on each surface of each cube, with the four excess surfaces being used for repeating one time each, the letters A, B, C, and D. Both upper-case and lower-case letters should be printed on each surface.

This game would proceed with each player casting the cube on the playing surface and attempting to arrange the letter appearing on the top surface of each cube in alphabetical order.

134

Scoring will be accomplished by the awarding of 1 point for each properly placed letter. Each player will have an equal number of turns, and the duration of the game will be determined at the outset as a defininte number of turns or a specified amount of time, still allowing for equal chances.

This game can also be used for simple identification of alphabet letters for students requiring this practice.

TITLE: COVER 6 (8)

PURPOSE: To develop dictionary skills.

ACTIVITY: Game.

PROCEDURE: Each student is given a chart like one of the following:

a	b	c	d	e	f		g	h	i	j	K	l
m	n	o	p	q	r	s	t	u	v	w	x	y	z

A stack of cards, each with a vocabulary word written on it, is placed in the middle of the table. Students take turns drawing cards one at a time. Each child then places his card on top of the appropriate letter (apple on a, boat on b, etc.).

If a player draws a card that he cannot use, he may trade with another player for a card that he *can* use.

The first person to cover six letters wins the game. After each game, the students should trade charts.

Note: Make sure there are an equal number of words for each letter.

TITLE: WORD QUIZ (9)

PURPOSE: Teaching dictionary skills.

ACTIVITY: Game.

PROCEDURE: Have each child choose an easy word such as *dog, cat, rat.* Using a dictionary, he prepares a list of words, beginning with his chosen word, and a clue to each answer. When the pupil gives the clue, the other students guess the answer. The first one to guess correctly wins 1 point. The pupil with the most points is declared the winner for the day.

Example: hat

1. A container for hats   hatbox
2. A small ax   hatchet

135

3. A maker of hats   hatter
4. A strong feeling   hate

TITLE: GOING PLACES   (10)

PURPOSE: To see if students know alphabetic order.

ACTIVITY: Group.

PROCEDURE: Say, "I am going to the zoo. Name the animals I will see alphabetically from A through Z."

    A. . . . aardvark
    B. . . . bear
    C. . . . chimpanzee
    D. . . . deer
    E. . . . elephant . . .

Variation—Peoples

    A. . . . Asians
    B. . . . Brazilians
    C. . . . Canadians
    D. . . . Danes
    E. . . . Egyptians

TITLE: ANY WORD WILL DO   (11)

PURPOSE: Dictionary skill.

ACTIVITY: Game.

PROCEDURE: This game can be played by groups of four to eight. The group is divided up into two equal teams. Each group is given a different-numbered list of letters. The object is for both teams to take turns calling out numbers to the opposing team. The teams then take the letters called, and placing them in any order, try to be the first to make a word and verify it with the dictionary.

TITLE: DICTIONARY RACE   (12)

PURPOSE: The purpose of this activity is to provide practice in locating words quickly.

ACTIVITY: Group.

PROCEDURE: Have the children arrange their desks in four rows. Place one dictionary on the first desk on each row. Space between rows should be great enough so that a child cannot see his neighbor's paper. Along with the dictionary, include a test sheet and one pencil. When the teacher signals the start of the game, each pupil will pick up his dictionary (four) and look up the word numbered one, write down the answer, and pass it to the person in back of him. He will look up the answer to the next question and write it down, passing it on, until each child in the row has had the dictionary. If the pencil breaks, he will raise his hand and the teacher will give him another. Tests will be scored not only on time, but also on accuracy. Variations can be used by starting the books at the back of each row or by alternating starting points on every other row.

TITLE: DICTIONARY BINGO   (13)

PURPOSE: To check the child's understanding of guide words and to give the child practice with alphabetization.

ACTIVITY: Game.

PROCEDURE: Each child receives a bingo card with 16 words on it, one in each square. The teacher calls out a pair of guide words from the dictionary. Each child looks for a word on his card that would be found on that page in the dictionary. The first person to cover four words in a straight line, either vertically, horizontally, or diagonally, wins.

The words for this game can be taken directly from the reading lesson. The children must know what guide words are, and they must know how to alphabetize.

Sample card: Sample guide words:

Aleut	key	comet	laugh
flint	mission	parka	Jacob
shine	hair	symbol	black
editor	attend	high	county

ability—anxiety
cooperate—dilemma
flimsy—gloat
supervise—tricorn
school—summer
parka—proud
approach—awful
conjure—comment, etc.

The guide words should be written on strips of heavy paper. These strips should be shown to the class as the guide words are called. In this way there will be no confusion as to the spelling and/or pronunciation of these words.

TITLE: GUIDE-WORD HUNT   (14)

PURPOSE: To provide practice in using guide words.

ACTIVITY: Game.

PROCEDURE: Teacher puts diagram such as the following on the board:

half	–	hat	hike	–	hive
	1			4	
have	–	help	hog	–	hot
	2			5	
herd	–	hide	hum	–	hut
	3			6	

The teacher makes a bingo card for each child, numbering all boxes randomly from 1 to 6.

R I N G O

The words for the drill should be written on 1" x 3" cards, and each contains a letter code–R, I, N, G, O–as a column designator.

The teacher draws the cards, calling out the word and letter code. The children use guide words to find where a given word would be located and mark the number corresponding to the particular page on their card, under the designated column only.

The first child to get RINGO is the winner.

TITLE: ALPHABET SCRAMBLE   (15)

PURPOSE: To give the child practice with alphabetization.

ACTIVITY: Game.

PROCEDURE: The new words from the reading lesson are written on individual strips of heavy paper. The strips are placed face down on the table. Initially, each child draws four strips from the center of the table. On each successive turn, the child draws one new card and places it in alphabetical order with the cards already drawn. The object of the game is for each child to alphabetize the words he has drawn from the pile. If a student errs in alphabetizing, he returns all strips to the center and waits his next turn before drawing four new strips. When all strips have been used, the student with the most words correctly alphabetized wins. (A single student may play by competing against time or against his previous achievement.)

ILLUSTRATION:

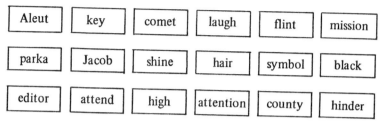

Aleut	key	comet	laugh	flint	mission
parka	Jacob	shine	hair	symbol	black
editor	attend	high	attention	county	hinder

TITLE: ABC GAME　　(16)

PURPOSE: To provide practice in using alphabetical order as a dictionary skill.

ACTIVITY: Group.

PROCEDURE: Compile a stack of word cards (approximately 100 or more if you wish). These words should be familiar to the students. Keep these cards face down. Divide the class into teams by making each row a team. Give each player in each team a card face down. They are not to turn it over or show it to anyone until the signal is given. At the signal, each team is to arrange themselves in alphabetical order. The first team to do so correctly receives 1 point. (You may want to put a time limit on the game.)

| travel | wish |

TITLE: ALPHABET SPEED　　(17)

PURPOSE: To increase dictionary speed and become familiar with synonyms and antonyms.

ACTIVITY: Game.

PROCEDURE: This game is to be played with the entire class. The class is divided into approximately five teams. Taking turns, one member from each team will compete against another in looking up a word in the dictionary when the instructor calls out a word. The object is for a team member to find

the word in the dictionary and then find either the synonym or antonym (the teacher will declare which) and write
the answer on the board. The student must be able to prove
his answer with the dictionary. The first to do so scores a
point for his team.

TITLE: WORD MEANING QUIZ (18)

PURPOSE: To practice dictionary skills and develop a wider vocabulary.

ACTIVITY: Group.

PROCEDURE: Each child should look up five words in the dictionary and
be very sure of their meanings. He should then write "yes"
or "no" type questions to test the meanings of the words,
such as:

An *autoharp* is a musical instrument?
Is a tiger a *coniferous* animal?

These questions should be written on separate cards with
the correct answer on the back. Divide the class into two
teams. Collect the prepared questions. The questions should
be alternated from one team to the other. There should be
only one chance to answer. The pupil must reply to his
"yes" or "no" answer by giving the meaning of the word. If
the player gets the word wrong, then the person who made
up the question should tell the class the meaning.

AN AUTOHARP IS A MUSICAL INSTRUMENT?

YES
(back)

TITLE: GETTING TO GRANNY'S HOUSE (19)

PURPOSE: To provide practice in using dictionary skills.

ACTIVITY: Group or independent.

PROCEDURE: The children need help getting to Granny's house. There are
various things they must do before they can get there. As
the children find the answers in the dictionary, let them
move a space at a time, or if they work in groups, all must
be completed before they can get to Granny's.

1. Find and list at least five animals in the A section
of your dictionary. Give the page number you
find them on. Example: ape, ant, asp, alligator, al-
paca, albatross, etc.

2. Give two different words listed above the word "bear" and two words following.
3. Look under "cap" ... and find a word that rhymes with "tape." What does it mean?
4. What is the word directly above the word "dawn"?
5. Write down two different definitions for the word "field."
6. What is the word that follows *glacis* and is before the word *gladden*. It means to be pleased _____ .
7. Are all of these words in the dictionary? Cat, dat, jat, lat, and mat.
8. What are two definitions of the word "jingle"?
9. What is a leash?
10. Is there a word that follows "zebra"?
11. Is there such a word as "lol" in your dictionary?
12. Find the word "making." What are the two guide words at the top of that page?
13. Our dictionary has more than just words and definitions. Name some other kinds of information it has.

TITLE: STUMP THE CLASS   (20)

PURPOSE: To encourage curiosity about words and *dictionary* use.

ACTIVITY: Group.

PROCEDURE: A child finds a word he thinks may stump the class. He looks up the word in the dictionary and makes it his own.

At game time, he tells the source (radio, TV, reading) and reads the dictionary definition to the class without telling the word. The class tries to guess the word. If they can't, he has a "stumper." He reveals it and adds it to a class chart, with the pronunciation and meaning and his own name.

It's a Stumper

Word	*Meaning*	*Name*
extinguish	to put out the flame to put an end to	John Brown

TITLE: DICTIONARY SLEUTHING   (21)

PURPOSE: To develop skill in using a dictionary.

ACTIVITY: Independent.

MATERIALS: Spelling word list and dictionaries.

PROCEDURE: The teacher gives students a list of spelling words. The students try to find the words in the dictionary. Then they must write the page number and definition in their own words. The teacher reviews their work in class.

TITLE: GUIDE-WORD SKILL   (22)

PURPOSE: Provide practice in using guide words.

ACTIVITY: Group.

PROCEDURE: The teacher puts hypothetical guide words on the board, such as could be found on four pages in a dictionary.

bat boat	heat horse	Mars mouse	tar turn

Each child is given an article or story and instructed to list as many words on each of the hypothetical pages as he is able to find in a specified time period. The child with the largest total of words in all four columns is the winner.

TITLE: DICTIONARY WORD SCRAMBLE   (23)

PURPOSE: This activity allows the child to employ his dictionary skills to use words in context.

ACTIVITY: Group or independent.

PROCEDURE: Give students words with which they are not familiar. Have the letters of the words scrambled. After each word, put

142

the page number it is found on in the dictionary. All students must use the dictionary. Have the children unscramble the words and locate them in the dictionary. Have them write meanings and then use the words in sentence context. *Skills Emphasized:* Dictionary skills.

Example: marf p. 302 farm—
eshou p. 403 house—
lbeta p. 896 table—

We visited our grandparents who have a *farm* in Virginia. Our *house* is the red brick one two stories tall. Tom put his books on the *table* when he came home from school.

TITLE: QUICK!   (24)

PURPOSE: To develop skill in finding answers quickly by skimming.

ACTIVITY: Individual.

MATERIALS: Individual copies of a short article or story (two or three paragraphs).

PROCEDURE: Each student is given a copy of the paragraphs face down. At the given signal, papers are turned over and the teacher asks the first question. Students skim for the answer and raise their hands when they have it.

ILLUSTRATION:

Teacher asks question.

Find answer.

Raise your hand.

8 Sharpening Comprehension Skills to Get Precision Understanding

• • • • • • • • • • • • • •

The goal in reading is comprehension, and while word recognition skills are helpful means to this end, these skills alone will not be enough for the reader to get total meaning. A fully functioning reader requires adequate command of comprehension skills as well.

Most reading programs contain quite a bit of word recognition development and have some comprehension activity, but most programs are without sufficient activities for adequate development of the various comprehension skills. In Chapters 8 and 9, you will find a multitude of ideas to assist you in providing adequate lessons for your students' comprehension skill development.

Five of the comprehension skills—finding the main idea, grasping details, following directions, remembering what is read, and critical reading—are covered in Chapter 8, and they follow in that order.

As in the preceding chapters, you will find games, group, and independent activities for each skill. Again, this will enable you to have a flexible program. While some students will need practice in finding the main idea, others will have this competency. You will find it easy to select an activity for one group while you work with another who might be deficient in grasping details. Of course, not all students will become competent in a particular skill at the same time, for some will need more practice than others. When additional practice is necessary, you can easily provide independent activities for those in need.

Whether the energizer is a game, group, or independent activity, it will be fun for your students to do. The built-in motivation that is intrinsic in these ideas will not only make your job more pleasant but also will facilitate your students' achievement.

TITLE: WHAT'S MISSING   (1)

PURPOSE: To develop the ability to find the main idea of a sentence and the acquisition of a broad vocabulary.

ACTIVITY: Game.

PROCEDURE: A selected paragraph is read by the members of the teams or by the individual student if only two students are playing. The paragraph may be created by the teacher or a student, taken from a newspaper, or copied out of a book. Important words in the paragraph are then removed or blackened. The student or the members of the teams then read the paragraph again and try to discover which words have been left out. Points can be scored for each word the player or team members have correctly identified as the missing words. The words taken out of the paragraph can include the main idea of the sentence, vocabulary words, and new words whose meanings can be found by the context of the paragraph.

ILLUSTRATION:

@NEW YORK LEDGER

WASHINGTON—The _____ , _____ is conducting an _____ program to develop _____ uses for atomic explosives that appear to American officials to be more _____ than the corresponding Plowshare program of the United States.

The Soviet program was described to American experts by the _____ at meetings held in Moscow last month and in Vienna this week.

Word Blanks: 1. Soviet Union
                  2. ambitious
                  3. peaceful
                  4. extensive
                  5. Russians

TITLE: TELEGRAM   (2)

PURPOSE: To develop skills in finding main ideas of sentences.

ACTIVITY: Group.

MATERIALS: Telegram blanks or ditto of a simulated telegram blank. Pencils.

Ditto of teacher-composed letter containing information about time and place of arrival, what clothes he or she should bring, whether someone will meet him or her at the station, etc. (A different letter should be written for the boys and girls.)

PROCEDURE: Children are to pretend that they have been invited to visit a friend for the weekend and have written a letter (the teacher's ditto), telling their friend when they will arrive, etc. Suddenly, they realize that the letter will not reach their friend in time so they need to send a telegram. Explain that you are charged by the word when you send a telegram so you must convey the main ideas of your letter in as few words as possible. Give some examples of what might occur if you fail to include all of the essential ideas. Then have the children read the letter, determine the main idea of each sentence, and write these on the telegram blank. When finished, the students who wish to, may read their telegrams out loud, and the class may discuss whether they included all of the main ideas and only the main ideas. Is he or she likely to be stranded at the station? At 5 cents a word, how much would it cost to send the telegram? Is there someone in the class who can send their telegram cheaper because they sent the same message in less words? Etc.

TITLE: CONTROL IDEAS   (3)

PURPOSE: To provide practice in finding the main idea of a paragraph.

ACTIVITY: Group.

PROCEDURE: The children are given a series of paragraphs to read where the main idea is indicated in large letters. The majority of the paragraphs should have the beginning sentence as the main idea. They are then given a paragraph and told to circle the same things that were in big print.

The teacher could have the paragraphs on individual pieces of paper for the children to look at. These could circulate around the class, and when sufficient time had been allowed for examining and reading them, they could be collected and a sheet of unmarked paragraphs handed out for working. The only directions could be to look at the unmarked paragraphs, but don't identify the bold print as the main idea. See if the students can pick it out for themselves and circle the main idea.

Example: One day while walking home from school, WE SAW A SQUIRREL IN A TREE. He was eating an acorn.

He would drop tiny pieces of it to the ground. While we watched, he jumped from branch to branch as if he were showing off.

WHY DO I LIKE SCHOOL? I like school because all my friends are there. I also have a very nice teacher who lets us sing and color.

After examining these paragraphs, give the following:

Last summer we took a camping trip to the mountains. We saw lots of animals and cooked on an open fire.

TITLE: REMEMBER ME   (4)

PURPOSE: Reading for main ideas.

ACTIVITY: Group.

PROCEDURE: Before starting, a story should be selected and the paragraphs numbered. Ask, "Are you a good hunter? If you are, you will be able to find each paragraph below. Write the page number of each paragraph on the lines and the number of the paragraph."

	Page	Paragraph Number
What John and Mary found	_____	_____
Why Mother said no	_____	_____
Who went home	_____	_____
What time was it	_____	_____
Where they slept	_____	_____

TITLE: FINDING THE MAIN IDEA   (5)

PURPOSE: To find the main idea.

ACTIVITY: Group or independent.

MATERIALS: Pencil, cards with se' cted paragraphs written on them.

PROCEDURE: The pupil will read the paragraph, find the main idea, choose the best title, and circle the correct number.

Example: It was a wonderful pie!
It made the whole kitchen smell good.
The crust was crisp and melted in the mouth.
The cherries were sweet and the dark, red juice oozed out over the plate.

Choose the best title:

(1) A Pretty Pie
(2) Pie for Lunch
(3) A Delicious Pie

149

TITLE: ARTISTIC SUMMARY   (6)

PURPOSE: To encourage the child to grasp the general subject matter of a specified reading material. One general drawing should cover the entire story.

ACTIVITY: Group or independent (mural).

MATERIALS: Art paper, crayons, paint (etc.), short fiction story.

PROCEDURE: Instruct the child to read selected short fiction and express the main idea of the story in a picture. Stress the idea of not using a series of pictures (describing details of the story). It may be a group project, with the entire class reading the same story and collaborating on the expression of the main theme for a class mural.

TITLE: LET'S BE A DETECTIVE   (7)

PURPOSE: To learn how to find the main idea of a paragraph.

ACTIVITY: Independent.

MATERIALS: Paragraphs cut into sentences.
Envelopes to keep each paragraph.

PROCEDURE: Several children could play and exchange envelopes. The children are to decide which sentence tells about all the others. Place this sentence at the top of the desk. Then place others underneath it to describe the main idea.

Example: (Since the paragraphs are cut into sentences, the order does not make any difference.)

Mrs. Green had many things to do before lunch. (main idea)
There was the cleaning to be picked up and the shopping to do.
Her shoes had to be dropped off to be fixed.
Then she had to be at the beauty shop by 11 o'clock.

Mr. Lane wanted a station wagon, but Mrs. Lane liked the two-door hardtops.
The two boys were interested only in the fancy racing cars.
Each one in the Lane family had a different idea about the car the family should have. (main idea)

Debbie got her pink dress out of the closet and put it on.
She splashed a little perfume on her favorite handkerchief.
Then, with a pretty smile, she started down the stairs.
She wanted to look her very best for the guests. (main idea)

The children were playing many games at school. (main idea)

John and Jim were playing catch.
Susan, Mary, and Joan were busy jumping rope.
Bill and Joe were playing hide-and-seek.
Other children were playing volleyball.

TITLE: CONCENTRATION   (8)

PURPOSE: To help students develop the ability to grasp details.

ACTIVITY: Small group game (two to four people).

MATERIALS: Two cards (on which pictures or phrases represent details) for each *set* of details. One card corresponds to details in a story, one does not. The title of the story is also on the front of the card.

PROCEDURE: Cards are in two stacks, face up. Each person takes a turn, at which time he must decide which card accurately represents the details in the story. To find the right answer, he turns the card over. On the back is the title of the story, the number of the set of two cards, and "yes" or "no" (depending on whether or not it represents the details accurately).

ILLUSTRATION:

Title "_____"	Title "_____"
Mary's red hair	Mary's brown hair

NO Title "_____" Set 3	YES Title "_____" Set 3

TITLE: MURAL COORDINATION   (9)

PURPOSE: Grasping details.

ACTIVITY: Game.

MATERIALS: One large mural with a farm scene, consisting of colors and animals the students have studied. (Students have already completed the artwork.)

PROCEDURE: After a week, cover the mural and have the students identify in detail the various items presented according to name and color. Students will correctly match colors with objects and write the words down to compile a spelling list.

After the students have completed the artwork for the construction of the mural, allow them to construct the mural in any fashion they may desire. Review their purpose for making the mural, and review the spelling words before covering the mural to test them on their recognition skills.

TITLE: **TIC-TAC-TOE FOR DETAILS** (10)

PURPOSE: To grasp details.

ACTIVITY: Game.

MATERIALS: Poster board or chart or area of blackboard to put tic-tac-toe game on.

PROCEDURE: The students will read a story. Then they will answer questions about the story by filling in x's and o's.

For example, the story is about a trip. These would be suggested questions: The correct answer will receive an x or o in the correct block. Three across in any direction wins!

ILLUSTRATION:

Who was the main character?	Where did he live?	How was he going to travel?
Why did he go?	What would he bring back?	How long would he be gone?
Who was his friend?	Where was he going?	When would he go?

TITLE: **READING FOR INFORMATION** (11)

PURPOSE: To improve the students' ability to extract information from reading.

ACTIVITY: Game.

MATERIALS: Copies for all students of a reading selection are needed. Also, for the game, the teacher should have prepared a set of questions on the reading selection. The answers to these questions should be very simple and brief.

PROCEDURE: Explain to the class that they are going to play a game in which they will win points by being the first to answer a question on the reading selection. Distribute the reading selection and allow the students time to read it. Next, divide the class into three or four teams, and send a member of each team to the blackboard. Allow them to take their reading selection with them. Ask them a question, and the first student to write the correct answer on the board wins a point for his team.

TITLE: EXTEMPORANEOUS "SPEECHES" (12)

PURPOSE: Grasping details.

ACTIVITY: Game.

PROCEDURE: Divide the class into teams or simply call on individuals. Ask a student to stand and give as much information as he can about any word or subject. He receives 1 point for each fact. If another student thinks he can give more, he must repeat what has already been given before he adds to it.

Example: In spelling—"Steven, tell us about the word catastrophe."

> The word catastrophe is a noun.
> It has four syllables.
> It means disaster.
> An antonym is "windfall."
> The accent is on the second syllable.
> It is spelled c-a-t-a-s-t-r-o-p-h-e.
> It has four vowels.
> It has seven consonants.
> It has one silent vowel.

Score: 9 points.

TITLE: REMEMBERING (13)

PURPOSE: Provide practice in remembering specific details of a story.

ACTIVITY: Game.

PROCEDURE: The teacher prepares questions on facts from a given story, writing each on a card. The class is divided into two teams, and the teacher reads an account to all, after which she randomly chooses cards and presents questions. The first team to answer correctly keeps the card. The winner is the team with the most cards collected after all have been presented.

TITLE: PICKY, TRICKY LISTENING (14)

PURPOSE: Grasping details and following directions.

ACTIVITY: Game.

MATERIALS: Self-prepared story.
Color chart.

153

PROCEDURE: Make up a simple story or use mine. Ask pupils to raise their hands, clap, etc. each time they hear a particular word. In my stories, I am stressing the color words. Be sure to write the key word on the board so students will recognize it when they see it again. Students should also be able to identify the color on the color chart.

The Little Red Hen put on her bright red apron and went out in her little red car. At Mr. Red's store, she bought some red apples and some red raspberries and some bananas. "Now, I will have lots of fruit to put in my little red basket," said the Little Red Hen. (RAISE RIGHT HAND ON RED)

Mr. Blue Jay flew up into the bright blue sky and into his nest in the blue fir tree. His blue-feathered babies were waiting for some blue worms, and some blue berries, and some bugs. "Now, we can fly for the first time to Mr. Blueworth's blue birdbath," said Daddy Blue Jay. (CLAP ON BLUE)

Curious George jumped on his yellow tricycle and rode into the hot, yellow sun. George was going to Charlie's pretty, yellow house where they planned to fly his new, yellow kite. When he arrived he was hungry, so Charlie gave him two yellow bananas, and two yellow pears, and then two glasses of milk. Now, the man with the yellow hat was angry because he couldn't find George. He was yelling all the way down the street, so Curious George jumped back on his yellow tricycle and rode home—very quickly. (STOMP FEET ON YELLOW)

TITLE: TREASURE HUNT   (15)

PURPOSE: To instruct the class in following directions.

ACTIVITY: Game for ten children or up to an entire class.

MATERIALS: Written clues in sequence and some type of token rewards for the winning group.

PROCEDURE: Divide the class into teams of five members. Have a separate set of sequential clues for each group, all clues leading to the same jackpot. Hide the clues in the appropriate places around the classroom. Each group should have a leader who does the actual searching. Groups sit together and help the leader solve the clues. Make it imperative for directions to be followed in order for the jackpot to be found. The first team to find the jackpot wins its contents.

Example of set of clues:

It is above the floor but below the ceiling.

Look around neither to the left nor right, forward nor backward if you have located the middle.

It is not immediately visible.

It is under something.

(Jackpot is in a desk centered in the room.)

TITLE: TELEVISION STORY TIME (16)

PURPOSE: To grasp details, to formulate conclusions, and for critical reading.

ACTIVITY: Group.

MATERIALS: A box with a window and two rods to make a television set.
Paper (8 x 11) for drawing pictures.
Crayons.
Tape to put the pictures in a roll.

PROCEDURE: Divide the group into pairs. Have each two children read one page of a story and draw a picture of what they have read. Have them think about what they are reading and grasp important details.

After all the pictures are drawn, tape or paste them together in a roll for the television set. Choose one child as a narrator to tell the story for the whole class.

ILLUSTRATION:

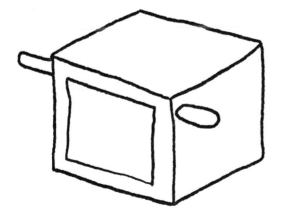

Title of Story
(1st)
(2nd)
(3rd)

Roll the pictures on the rod.

TITLE: TURTLES   (17)

PURPOSE: To develop the comprehension skill of picking out the important details in a paragraph.

ACTIVITY: Group.

PROCEDURE: Illustrate the details that are to be remembered from a paragraph and discuss the illustrations before the paragraph is read. Have the student read the paragraph and the questions, remembering the important details from the paragraph.

Turtles

There are many kinds of turtles, living in many different countries. From the tiniest to the largest of 1,000 pounds, they are all interesting. All turtles have bodies covered with scales. They can live on both land and water. When a turtle is frightened, it pulls its head, legs, and tail into its shell for safety. All turtles hatch from eggs. After the mother turtle lays her eggs in the sand, she covers them with earth and leaves to keep them warm until they hatch. As soon as the baby turtles hatch, they hurry toward the water, where they feel safer from their enemies. In the water, the young turtles feed on insects and small water animals. They grow fast, and each scale of the boxlike shell adds a new, wide rim every summer. By counting the rims, you can tell how old a growing turtle is.

1. The bodies of turtles are covered with: a. fins b. scales c. hard plates

2. Turtles live: a. on the land only b. in the water only c. on the land and in the water

3. A turtle pulls its head, legs, and tail into its shell when it is: a. mad b. sleepy c. frightened d. eating

4. The mother turtle: a. sits on her eggs until they hatch b. covers her eggs with sand and leaves c. carries her eggs in her shell

156

5. In the water, young turtles feed on: a. insects b. plants c. pieces of shell

6. The rims on the shell of the turtle tell the turtle's: a. size b. age c. color d. speed

TITLE: LAND HO!   (18)

PURPOSE: To develop the comprehension skill of picking out the important details in a paragraph.

ACTIVITY: Group.

PROCEDURE: Illustrate and label the important details from a selected passage the child is to read and have the child discuss the illustrations. The child will then read the paragraph and answer the questions, remembering the details.

Land Ho!

When the sailors on the ships the Pinta, Nina, and Santa Maria looked over the rail and down at the green water, they saw signs of land. A slender green reed, a wooden pole, a small board, and a branch with berries on it, went floating by. Small land birds, called sandpipers, were flying overhead. All of this happened on Thursday, October 11, 1492.

It was not so surprising, then, that Rodrigo de Triana, a sailor on the ship Pinta, soon saw land. At two o'clock in the morning on October 12, in full moonlight, he saw the low-lying dark mass on the horizon. By noon of the same day, the crew set foot on the sandy beach. This is the way the discovery of America was recorded nearly 500 years ago in the journal written by Christopher Columbus—the admiral of the three little vessels.

1. Pinta and Nina were the names of two: a. sailors b. ships c. cities

2. Where were the pole and branch with berries? a. on the beach b. in the water c. on the ship

3. On what date was land first sighted? a. October 12 b. October 11 c. November 12

4. Where did Columbus record this news? a. on the radio b. in his journal c. in a paper

157

TITLE: FROM HORSES TO JETS   (19)

PURPOSE: To develop the comprehension skill of picking out the important details in a paragraph.

ACTIVITY: Group.

PROCEDURE: Illustrate the objects that will be the basis for the details to be remembered from a selected reading. Have the child discuss the objects and then read the selection and answer the questions, remembering the details.

From Horses to Jets

There have been many changes in means of land travel in this country. The early settlers traveled by horseback. They rode over the Indian trails, through dense forests. Later, roads were widened and stagecoaches were brought over from England. By 1756, a regular stage route was running between Boston, New York, and Philadelphia.

A hundred years went by. Railroad trains steamed across the country. Slowly they pushed all the way to California. Then, as the twentieth century opened, automobiles appeared on the roads. It was a number of years before many families owned automobiles. But once they did, more traveled in their cars than by train.

Now air travel is taking the lead over all forms of land and sea travel. In 1960, for the first time, more people crossed the Atlantic by plane than by ship.

1. The first settlers in America traveled by: a. horseback b. car c. wagon d. plane

2. When was the first stagecoach route running? a. 1956 b. 1620 c. 1756 d. 1960

3. About how much later were railroad trains in use? a. 100 years b. 500 years c. 200 years

4. What now carries more families than trains do? a. automobiles b. stagecoaches c. buses d. planes

5. What took the lead in travel in 1960? a. cars b. rockets c. planes d. ships

TITLE: PAPER BAG DRAMA   (20)

PURPOSE: To give children a reason to find the main ideas of a story and for grasping details.

ACTIVITY: Group.

MATERIALS: Paper bag, crayons, scissors, paste, construction paper.

PROCEDURE: Children read a story and write a short play based on what they remember about the story.

They make puppets to represent the characters in the story and act out the play.

Puppets—take a paper bag, lunch size, and fold the bottom over. Out of construction paper, the children should make the head, and hat, if any, and the face, up to the upper lip. The bottom lip and beard, or collar, is made out of a separate piece of construction paper. Using crayons, the children draw in the features.

When the puppets are made, the students are ready to perform the play.

TITLE: DETAIL LISTENING   (21)

PURPOSE: To develop skill in listening for details as a prelude to reading for details.

ACTIVITY: Group or independent (if earphones are available).

MATERIALS: Record player, earphones (optional), and descriptive records of interest to children. Tape might be used instead of records. Copies of questions.

PROCEDURE: Tell the children you are going to play a record and they are to listen carefully. Read over the questions and ask them to listen for the answers. After the record has finished, allow time for the children to complete their papers.

Record to be used: "It Was a One-Eyed, One-Horned, Flying Purple People-Eater"

Questions: 1. What did the animal look like? Draw a picture of him and color it.

            2. What did the little animal want to do?

            3. Did he do what he wanted? What happened at the end of the record?

159

TITLE: IS IT TRUE?   (22)

PURPOSE: The student will demonstrate his skill at grasping details by filling in answer blanks with the appropriate word.

ACTIVITY: Group.

MATERIALS: A writing utensil.
A short story.
An answer sheet with true and false statements on it.
A place to put *yes* and *no*.

PROCEDURE: Read aloud a short story about something the class has been studying. Pass out sheets with true and false statements and have the children write *yes* or *no* next to each statement.

Variations: A story could be included on a sheet of paper with true and false statements on it.

Example: The story is about the sun. It gives factual information concerning the sun. Statements about the story might be:

1. You could live on the sun. _____

2. The sun is a big star. _____

3. The earth is bigger than the sun. _____

4. The sun is burning hot. _____

5. The sun is highest in early morning. _____

TITLE: WORDS IN A PUZZLE   (23)

PURPOSE: To provide practice in finding details.

ACTIVITY: Independent.

MATERIALS: A rectangle puzzle with specific words hidden in it.

PROCEDURE: The child tries to find the words in a given list in the puzzle. Words are formed by moving vertically or horizontally.

ILLUSTRATION:

Household Items

A	B	E	D	X	C	H	A	I	R
P	A	N	F	D	A	E	R	R	U
R	N	L	S	O	N	A	M	E	G
O	I	C	I	O	D	T	C	A	R
N	S	A	A	R	L	E	H	D	L
A	T	T	I	C	E	R	A	B	A
L	E	T	R	U	N	K	I	A	M
M	R	T	S	I	N	K	R	T	P

Find:

Apron	Rug
Banister	Pan
Bed	Can
Chair	Sink
Armchair	Cat
Trunk	Lamp
Read	Bat

160

PURPOSE: To teach different skills, including grasping details, finding main ideas, formulating conclusions, and critical reading.

ACTIVITY: Independent.

MATERIALS: Mimeographed sheets of the type illustrated below (though letters may be placed in any order).

Reading assignments followed by questions (multiple choice) which would evaluate the desired skill. Choices for the questions would be lettered rather than numbered, as explained below.

Crayons, paints, marking pens, or some other media for filling in the squares.

PROCEDURE: The student reads the assignment and answers the questions by filling in the square that corresponds to the correct answer. When he is finished, the colored squares will form a picture, a letter, a number, etc., or, by unscrambling the colored letters, they will form a word. The answer (that is, what is formed) could be given at the end of the questions or on the back of the page, so that the student could check his work.

ILLUSTRATION:

1. Johnny's favorite shirt was:
   (F_1) the blue one
   (H_2) the checked one
   (Y_2) the one with the missing button

A_1	B_1	C_1	D_1	E_1	F_1	G_1
H_1	I_1	J_1	K_1	L_1	M_1	N_1
O_1	P_1	Q_1	R_1	S_1	T_1	U_1
V_1	W_1	X_1	Y_1	Z_2	A_2	B_2
C_2	D_2	E_2	F_2	G_2	H_2	I_2
J_2	K_2	L_2	M_2	N_2	O_2	P_2
Q_2	R_2	S_2	T_2	U_2	V_2	W_2
X_2	Y_2	Z_2	A_3	B_3	C_3	D_3
E_3	F_3	G_3	H_3	I_3	J_3	K_3
L_3	M_3	N_3	O_3	P_3	Q_3	R_3
S_3	T_3	U_3	V_3	W_3	X_3	Y_3

A_1	B_1	C_1	D_1	E_1	F_1	G_1
H_1		J_1	K_1		M_1	N_1
O_1		Q_1	R_1		T_1	U_1
V_1		X_1	Y_1		A_2	B_2
C_2						I_2
J_2	K_2	L_2	M_2		O_2	P_2
Q_2	R_2	S_2	T_2		V_2	W_2
X_2	Y_2	Z_2	A_3		C_3	D_3
E_3	F_3	G_3	H_3		J_3	K_3
L_3	M_3	N_3	O_3		Q_3	R_3
S_3	T_3	U_3	V_3	W_3	X_3	Y_3

TITLE: MAGNIFICO PINATA   (25)

PURPOSE: Following directions and grasping details.

MATERIALS: (1) Pinata.
(2) Paper animals.

ACTIVITY: Game.

PROCEDURE: The students will construct the pinata and cut out various animals from construction paper to put in it. Ask the students to identify the various animals and the sounds they make. The students should then be able to name the animals and match them with their sounds. The students should also be able to write the correct names of the animals and be able to match them with their names when asked to do so.

Example: Divide the class into two groups, instructing one group to hold up an animal and call on one of their classmates to identify it by making its sound and naming it. Have the groups reverse their assignments and repeat the drill. Ask the students to write the names of the animals on paper as they hear a recording of their sounds on a tape recorder.

TITLE: EVERYDAY ACTIVITIES   (26)

PURPOSE: This exercise is to teach the child to follow directions by making pictures of everyday activities. Reading and comprehension are reinforced by the picture.

ACTIVITY: Game, group, independent—the activity is done by a group and can be made into a game by letting children decide who makes the picture cards best.

MATERIALS: Construction paper, scissors, paste, crayons or magazine pictures.

PROCEDURE: Direct the children to fold the paper in half widthwise. Show them how to divide it into equal parts, depending on the size of the picture desired. Have topics such as "A Toy I Like" or "What I do at Bedtime," etc. Have them print this on the front of the card. On the inside, have the child draw a picture to describe his title, or cut an appropriate one from a magazine and paste it inside.

ILLUSTRATION:

TITLE: SIGN LANGUAGE   (27)

PURPOSE: Too often children are given explicit directions on how to do something, but they do not read carefully or realize that the work is completed by a step-by-step process. This exercise is designed to show children how to decode a story using symbols, thereby reinforcing how to follow directions.

ACTIVITY: Group.

MATERIALS: The sheets may be mimeographed, or, if children are mature enough, they may copy the chart and message on construction paper and perhaps draw a picture of the completed story with crayons.

PROCEDURE: Give the children the following instructions:
Follow the language clues given in the box with the heading SIGN LANGUAGE and find out what the message below means. Write the message on the blank lines. The teacher may make up her own story and set of symbols.

ILLUSTRATION:

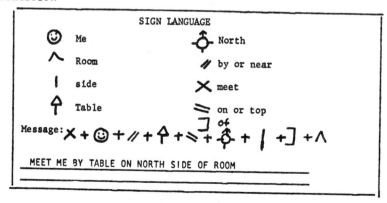

163

TITLE: A LISTENING ADVENTURE   (28)

PURPOSE: To learn to follow directions.

ACTIVITY: Group or independent.

MATERIALS: Tape recorder and reader, or any book that contains stories, ditto sheet, and crayons.

PROCEDURE: The teacher will record a story from a reader or from a book of stories. After the children hear the complete story, the tape is stopped so the teacher can distribute a set of ditto papers and a crayon to each child. On the papers, should be a multiple-choice set of pictures or words about specific events which the children are to recall from the story. (When the tape is started again, children will hear directions for marking their papers.) Directions should be given only once.

Example: A group which needed to improve oral reading speed and developmental reading skills followed along in the text as the story was placed once again on the recorder. The teacher would stop the tape and help the children associate the printed punctuation symbols with inflectional tones.

TITLE: FOLLOWING DIRECTIONS   (29)

PURPOSE: To stress the importance of following directions.

ACTIVITY: Group or independent.

MATERIALS: 1. Drawing paper.
           2. Crayons.

PROCEDURE: Introduce the lesson by making a general statement on the importance of following directions: "When your brother makes a model airplane, he must read directions to find out how to do it. When you help your mother cook, she tells you what to do and you listen to her directions. She may read in a cookbook to find how to make something good. It's important to do just what the directions say. Listen carefully and see how well you can follow directions."

"Jump twice on your right foot and sit down."
(Evaluate this before going on to the next.)

"Write your name on the board and turn around three times."

Guide the children in a discussion of good ways to follow directions. "It is important to listen to or read all the directions before starting out. Careful reading or listening is needed."

Have the children read one-sentence directions from the board. Then have a child erase the sentence and carry out the directions. The group may evaluate his actions.

Smile at a friend and take his hand.

Stand behind your chair and whistle two times.

Prepare directions on paper for individual work. Each begins with a general statement of what is wanted and goes on to give details. When the work is completed, let the children exhibit their work and discuss it.

1. Make a big clock.
   Put the minute hand at one.
   Then put the little hand at seven.

2. There is a little black train waiting to go over a mountain. Make a mountain with tracks for the train to go on. Make the train, too.

3. Make a circus ring. Put a ringmaster in it. Make three bears doing a funny dance around him. Put a funny hat on each bear.

4. There is a park in the city. Make two cages in the park. Put two bears in the first cage. Put one lion in the next cage.

TITLE: MAKING A COOKBOOK   (30)

PURPOSE: To learn the importance of following directions.

ACTIVITY: Individual or small group.

MATERIAL: White unruled paper cut about 6" x 8", ruler, pencil, magic markers, colored construction paper for book cover, simple recipes clipped from magazines.

PROCEDURE: Children select a recipe for favorite food. They write each direction separately and illustrate it. Then they make a booklet, designing their own cover, etc.

Example: Draw a measuring cup, marking measurements on it. Draw measuring spoons, cake pans, etc. Draw a decorated cake. Write the story of the cake (if for a party, or a special holiday, etc.). Read the story to the class. Encourage children to use dialogue in their stories and read orally with proper emphasis.

TITLE: REMEMBER   (31)

PURPOSE: For pupils who need practice in following directions.

ACTIVITY: Group or independent activity.

Make out mimeographed sheets or write on board and have pupils do as directed. Directions such as the following may be used.

1. Beginning with N, write the letters back to A.
2. Draw a 2-inch square and put an X in the center.
3. Turn to page 10 in your dictionary and copy the two guide words.
4. Write the number of boys and the number of girls in your classroom.

Example: Beginning with F, write the letters back to
B: F E D C B

TITLE: THE MAP   (32)

PURPOSE: This activity helps the child to learn to follow directions through map reading. He must be able to read the text with full understanding and have mastered the skill of noting details before he will be able to orient himself on the map.

ACTIVITY: Group or independent.

MATERIALS: One copy of exercise for each child.

PROCEDURE: Tell the children beforehand that they are going to learn to sketch a route on a map from a description listed below the map.

1. Look at the map first.
2. Read the text below and fill in the answers on the line from the map.

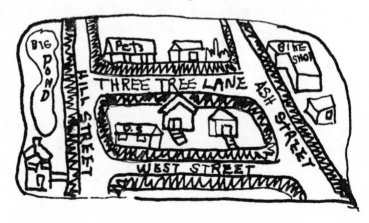

Jack lives next to the drugstore.
On what street does he live?
Jack lives on _____

166

Mr. Smith lives on the same block where the pet store is.

On what street does Mr. Smith live?

Mr. Smith lives on _____

Jan and Jill live next to the bike shop.

On what street do they live?

They live on _____

Pam lives on Hill Street.

She lives next to _____

TITLE: COLOR THE BALLOONS   (33)

PURPOSE: Following directions.

ACTIVITY: Group.

MATERIALS: Paper and crayons.

PROCEDURE: The children draw eight balloons like the sample below on their paper. Number the balloons 1 to 8. The children color the balloons according to the key.

ILLUSTRATION: *Key*

1. Blue	5. Brown
2. Green	6. Black
3. Yellow	7. Orange
4. Red	8. Purple

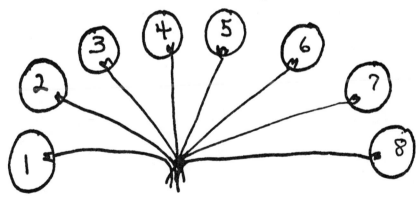

TITLE: BLINDMAN   (34)

PURPOSE: Practice in giving and following directions.

ACTIVITY: Group.

PROCEDURE: Blindfold one child. Select an object in the room and have another child direct the one who is blindfolded to the object without allowing him to bump into anything.

TITLE: PARTY FAVORS   (35)

PURPOSE: To improve listening skills and the ability to follow directions.

ACTIVITY: Group.

MATERIALS: Ditto of following patterns, construction paper, scissors,
glue, nut cups.

PROCEDURE: Teacher orally gives following directions step by step.

1. Trace and cut from construction paper the patterns you've been given.

2. Color in eyes, nose, and mouth lines.

3. Glue tail to body (illustrate how to children).

4. Bend legs and forearms forward along dotted
lines.

5. Glue acorn to forepaws.

6. Fasten nut cup to back of tail with glue.

TITLE: I'M LOST   (36)

PURPOSE: To develop skill in giving clear and accurate directions.

ACTIVITY: Group.

MATERIALS: Map (see illustration).

PROCEDURE: 1. Provide children with map shown.
2. Children take turns at being lost by telling where they are and where they want to be.
3. Person lost asks someone for directions.
4. If person can give clear and accurate directions, he is then the lost one seeking directions.

ILLUSTRATION:

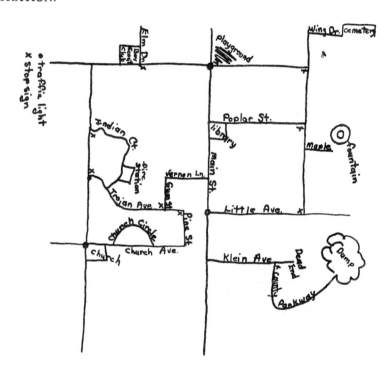

TITLE: LETTERS   (37)

PURPOSE: To give students manual practice in following verbal directions correctly.

ACTIVITY: Group.

DIRECTIONS: On your drawing paper, write the letters in the same position you see them on the board. I shall then read the directions aloud for you to follow.

169

MATERIALS: Children will need drawing paper and pencils. Draw on the blackboard the letters in positions shown below.

A	H	D
F	B	G
E	I	C

PROCEDURE:
1. Draw a large figure eight starting at A, going around C, and crossing at B.

2. Draw a square around F. Draw a square around I. Connect these squares with a straight line.

3. Draw a straight line from E to D, passing through B.

4. Write the figure 1 between A and H. Write the figure 3 between F and B. Write the figure 2 between E and I. Using a straight line, connect 1 with 2, passing through 3.

5. Starting at H, use broken line (---) and mark the way to D. Continuing with a broken line, mark the way to G from D. From G, using broken line, mark to H. The design should have the shape of a triangle.

6. Write the figure 3 between G and C. Write the figure 4 between I and C. Using an oblong circle, enclose these two numbers.

ILLUSTRATION:

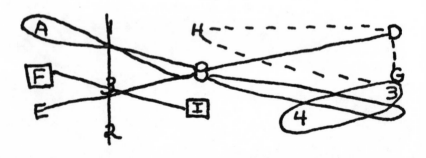

TITLE: READ AND DO   (38)

PURPOSE: Corrective practice for deficiencies in following directions.

ACTIVITY: Independent.

MATERIALS: Paper and crayons.

PROCEDURE: Pupils are given a number of directions to carry out.

Example: 1. Draw a house.

2. Put three windows in the house.

3. Put two panes of glass in each window.

4. Draw a chimney on the right-hand side of the roof.

5. Color the chimney brown.

6. Color the house red.

7. Draw a circle on the bottom right-hand side of your paper.

8. Now draw a square around the circle.

TITLE: DO WHAT I SAY   (39)

PURPOSE: To offer practice in reading simple paragraphs and following directions.

ACTIVITY: Independent.

MATERIALS: Since this is an independent activity, the teacher needs only to ditto the material on a work sheet. Class discussion could follow the activity.

PROCEDURE: The teacher should give only a simple direction, such as "Read and follow directions."

Example: Sample of format to be used.

A. This story is about Simpleton. He was the youngest son of a great king. He did not have much to say. That is why his brothers thought he was stupid.

1. Draw a line under the name of the youngest son.

2. Make a box around the words that tell what his father was.

3. Draw a line around the word that tells what his brothers thought Simpleton to be.

B. The sick king wanted to find out which of his sons should rule the country. He asked his three sons to do three things. They had to get the most beautiful carpet, the most beautiful ring, and the most beautiful princess in all the world.

1. Make a box around the words that tell what the sons had to bring home first.

2. Draw a line under the word that tells what was the matter with the king.

3. Draw a line around the word that tells how many sons the king had.

171

TITLE: DO-IT-YOURSELF PROJECTS   (40)

PURPOSE: To help teach students how to put directions in sequence. If the students follow the directions, the individual student can easily make Peanut Butter Cookies or stilts. Students have a choice.

ACTIVITY: Independent.

MATERIALS: Ingredients listed in the recipe or the materials required to make stilts.

PROCEDURE: First, have the students put the scrambled directions in sequence. Then explain that these two items can be made at home if they follow the directions.

Peanut Butter Cookies

2 cups graham cracker crumbs (about 24 crackers)
1 cup sugar
¾ cup evaporated milk
¾ cup chunk-style peanut butter
shortening

MATCHING:

1.____(a) Drop the dough by teaspoonfuls onto greased cookie sheets (use a butter knife to push the mixture off the spoon). Bake about 15 minutes, or until cookies puff up slightly but are still cool. Cool before removing from cookie sheets.

2.____(b) In a large bowl, mix the crumbs with sugar, evaporated milk, and peanut butter. Stir until well-blended.

3.____(c) Makes about 4 dozen cookies.

4.____(d) Crush graham crackers into very fine crumbs by placing the crackers between 2 sheets of waxed paper, and going over them with a rolling pin.

5.____(e) Turn on oven; set at 350 degrees. Grease cookie sheets with shortening.

Ken was coming over to see Barbie and she decided to make some cookies. The page was torn out and this is the way the directions read. Can you help unscramble the directions?

How to Make Stilts Out of Wood

2 lengths of wood
2 small blocks of wood for foot-rests
Nails

1. _____(a) Nail a foot-rest to each of the stilts.

2. _____(b) To walk on these stilts, pass the upper ends under your arms, grasp them about the middle, and climb onto the foot-rests.

3. _____(c) Cut the lengths of wood a little longer than your height.

P.S.: It will be easier to walk if you hold the stilts with your palms at the back and your thumbs in front, pointing downwards. Stand up straight and walk, taking short steps.

TITLE: WHAT DOES THE MONSTER LOOK LIKE?   (41)

PURPOSE: The student will demonstrate his skill at following directions by drawing a picture from a sheet of directions.

ACTIVITY: Independent.

MATERIALS: One piece of drawing paper.
Crayons in assorted colors.
One mimeographed sheet of directions.

PROCEDURE: The teacher makes up a funny description of a monster. The child reads this description and draws a picture from it.

Example: My body is round. It is purple. I have two heads. They are orange. One head has three eyes and one head has four eyes. I do not have any noses. I have two ears on each head. They are green. They are very large. I have one mouth in each head. Each mouth has only two sharp, pointy teeth. One tooth is yellow and the other is black. I have two arms and two hands. They are blue. Each hand has three fingers. I have three legs, with one foot on each leg. They are red. Each foot has seven toes. Draw me.

Each student is to include as many details as he can remember.

ILLUSTRATION:

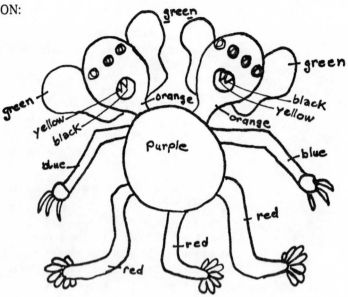

TITLE: CITY STREETS   (42)

PURPOSE: Following directions.

ACTIVITY: Independent.

MATERIALS: Crayons and mimeographed picture.

PROCEDURE: Give each child a copy of the mimeograph of a city street. Tell them that they are to follow all of the directions that are given. Then give them instructions such as: (1) put an X on the tallest building; (2) put 2X's on another building; (3) draw a circle around the bus; (4) draw a line connecting the policeman, the stoplight, and the bus.

ILLUSTRATION:

TITLE: PICTURE-STORY MATCHING   (43)

PURPOSE: Following directions.

174

ACTIVITY: Independent.

PROCEDURE: Write a story on the board which asks the children to do several things. Go over the story with them, and then have them draw a picture to match the story. The story can reinforce any new words or concepts that the children have learned.

ILLUSTRATION: DRAW A SET OF NINE 🌲 S.

COLOR FOUR GREEN.

COLOR FIVE BLUE.

DRAW A CIRCLE AROUND EACH 🌲

TITLE: READING TO LEARN A NEW ART SKILL   (44)

PURPOSE: The purpose of this activity is to improve the ability to follow written directions. The motivation for the students to read is the learning of a new art technique.

ACTIVITY: Group instructions for an independent activity.

MATERIALS: In the illustration, materials for a collage will be used—a 16" x 22" piece of construction paper (any color), either torn pieces of construction paper or pages from magazines which have been torn, and paste. Also needed are a reading selection on how to construct a collage (copies for everyone in class) and a set of questions on the reading selection (copies for everyone in class). Students who are more capable may be given a reading selection on the same topic but on a higher level. Also, a different set of questions would accompany a different reading selection.

PROCEDURE: The teacher explains to the class that they are going to learn a new art technique. She passes around the reading selection with questions attached. Next, she explains to them that after they have read the selection and answered the questions, they should raise their hands and she will check over the answers to the questions with them, answering any questions they might have about making a collage. Then, if they have answered the questions satisfactorily, they may get materials to begin work on their collage.

The answers to the questions are one-word answers or true-false, so that the teacher may review the answers quickly. As each student completes his questions to the satisfaction of the teacher, he may begin work, either at the desk or at an art table, on a collage. Those students who finish their questions first may make more than one collage or perhaps

175

be allowed time to spend on an activity such as free reading.

TITLE: PARK DETAILS   (45)

PURPOSE: Learning to follow directions by reading.

ACTIVITY: Independent.

PROCEDURE: Each sentence names something in Woodland Park. Draw a picture of each thing on the map.

1. Three cars are parked north of Route 7.
2. A bus is going west on Route 7.
3. Six trees are on the north side of Laughing Brook.
4. A deer is south of Duck Pond.
5. A boat is west of Boat Island.
6. A building is west of Round Hill.
7. A barn is on the south of the farm.
8. A cow is east of the barn.
9. Four children are walking west on Woodland Trail.
10. A car is east of the bus.

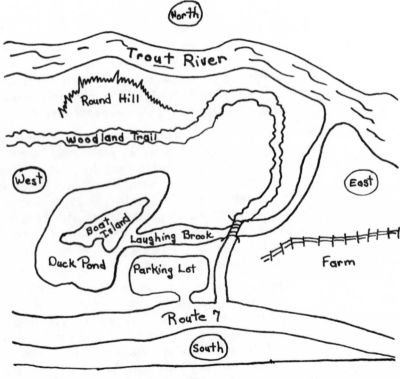

176

TITLE: DO AS I SAY   (46)

PURPOSE: Following directions.

ACTIVITY: Independent.

PROCEDURE:
1. Write the word "bear" under the picture of this animal.
2. Make the clock say 4 o'clock.
3. Color the flower red.
4. The bird is hungry. Put a worm in its mouth.
5. There are three pigs in the picture. Make marks under the picture to show how many pigs there are.

This exercise could be given orally or done on ditto sheets for practice in following written directions.

ILLUSTRATION:

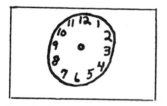 

TITLE: QUESTIONS AND ANSWERS   (47)

PURPOSE: To motivate students to remember what they read.

ACTIVITY: Group game.

PROCEDURE: The class is divided into two teams. The teacher has prepared two sets of cards, one with questions and one with answers, pertaining to a story the students have read. The teacher shows one of the questions (or answer cards). The student with the correct answer goes to the front of the room and reads his answer. Both teams have the same cards, so the one who realizes he has the correct answer first raises his hand for recognition. He then receives 1 point for recognition, and 1 point for correctly reading the response. The team with the most points when the teacher runs out of cards is the winner.

Questions and responses can be about story incidents, character identification, time sequence of a plot, etc. The game can be reversed by having the teacher hold up the answers, while the students respond with the questions.

ILLUSTRATION:

TITLE: SIMON SAYS   (48)

PURPOSE: To check story comprehension.

ACTIVITY: Group game.

PROCEDURE: After the class has completed reading their daily assigned story, this game can be played.

The teacher has all of the children stand by their desks while she stands in the front and acts as Simon. She may say, "Simon says take one step forward if Jane and Dick are brother and sister." According to the story, if this were true, the children should move. Those that don't step forward have to sit down.

The game continues, with her asking questions pertaining to the story until there is one child left standing. He then may be Simon.

TITLE: PICTURE COMPREHENSION   (49)

PURPOSE: To use pictures to develop comprehension skills.

ACTIVITY: Group.

PROCEDURE: Using an overhead projector and transparencies, the teacher can duplicate pictures from a story and ask the class to put them in the correct sequence, or write what was happening in the picture. It is always more fun to add a few similar pictures not in that story. Many activities of this nature can be used with the overhead projector.

TITLE: "CRITICAL THINKING" (50)

PURPOSE: To help children develop critical thinking abilities.

ACTIVITY: Game.

MATERIALS: Materials needed are several cards containing a different statement and a generalization formed from the statement.

PROCEDURE: The class can be divided into two teams. Each player on both teams is given a card similar to those below. The student must stand and read his card to the entire class and tell them whether the card is incorrect or correct. After this has been done, the student must give an explanation of why the card is incorrect or correct—in other words, justify his answer. A point is given each time a student is correct. If the other team points out why he is incorrect in his justification, then they receive the point.

ILLUSTRATION:

> 1. The U.S. flag is red, white, and blue.
>   (Fact or statement)
>
>   All flags are red, white, and blue.
>   (Generalization)

> 2. The teacher yelled at his class.
>
>   All teachers yell at their classes.

> 3. The man jogs every morning and is in perfect physical condition.
>
>   Jogging helps keep a person in good physical condition.

> 4. Paper clips hold papers tightly when they are 2" in length.
>
>   Two inches is a good length for paper clips.

TITLE: FACTO BINGO (51)

PURPOSE: To help the student learn critical evaluation.

ACTIVITY: Game.

MATERIALS: Game board and discs, which can be either round or square. The students could make their own game boards and discs.

PROCEDURE: The moderator (or instructor) reads the sentences. Each player must decide whether the statement is *fact* or *opinion* and places a disc over the appropriate square. The winner then becomes moderator for the next game. Any Bingo game is usable; i.e., cover all, diagonal coverage, etc.

ILLUSTRATION:

F	O	F	O
O	F	O	F
F	O	F	O
O	F	O	F

SAMPLE STATEMENTS:
Pepsi is best. (O)
Coke is a safe drink. (F)
The President acted wisely. (O)
America is a super power. (F)

TITLE: YOU BE THE JUDGE   (52)

PURPOSE: Distinguishing fact from opinion.

ACTIVITY: Group.

PROCEDURE: Cut out interesting pictures or advertisements and paste on 8½" x 11" construction paper. On the reverse side, write the heading FACT OR OPINION? Then list several statements about the picture, some factual and some opinions.

Each student comes up before the "judge" one at a time and takes a picture from the stack. The "judge" holds the picture so the "defendant" can see it and so the "judge" can read the statements. If the "defendant" answers all questions correctly, he then becomes the "judge." If he answers incorrectly, he is told to go back to jail (return to his seat).

ILLUSTRATION:

FACT OR OPINION?

1. There are two boys. (fact)

2. The dog is biting one of the boys. (opinion)

3. The boys just got out of school. (opinion)

4. There is a green lunch box on the ground. (fact)

TITLE: TV JINGLE   (53)

PURPOSE: To provide the students with an opportunity to practice reading critically and choosing fact from opinion.

ACTIVITY: Group.

PROCEDURE: Let the children make a list of their favorite television commercial jingles. (There will probably be hundreds of suggestions, but choose the best ones or one jingle from each child.) Copy these on a ditto sheet and give each child one sheet. Let them go through and circle the word or words which make the jingle questionable, or have them write under the jingle what is untrue about it.

Example: "Winston tastes good like a cigarette should." (Besides the poor grammar, answers could range from "How should a cigarette taste?", "Do you eat cigarettes?", or they could just underline the word *taste*.)

"Coke—It's the real thing."
(Does *real* mean it's alive? Is it the *only* real thing?, etc.)

Caution: The teacher will have to be selective in choosing the jingles for use. They should be of a questionable nature so that the students will have to read them and think about what they read.

TITLE: THE FOOLERS   (54)

PURPOSE: To help foster children's critical reading ability.

ACTIVITY: Group.

MATERIALS: Magazine and newspaper articles, scrapbooks, bulletin board.

PROCEDURE: Begin with a discussion about propaganda. List six or seven types. Next, give each child an example of one of the propaganda categories and have him figure out which type of propaganda it is. The children could bring in magazine and newspaper articles, letters to the editor, etc. and make scrapbooks with several pages for each type of propaganda. The class could also make an interesting bulletin board.

9 Succoring Study Skill Development for General and Specialized Use

• • • • • • • • • • • • •

Included in this chapter are energizers for teaching the skills of understanding sequence, formulating conclusions, building sentences, and developing oral reading fluency. The topics follow in the order given, group and independent activities providing you with many ideas for individualizing your instruction to meet students' skill needs.

Finding ideas for teaching comprehension and study skills is important and often frustrating to teachers. That teaching these skills is necessary is beyond question since any definition of reading includes getting literal meaning, interpreting what is read, and reacting to it. Teachers are aware of this and realize they have a responsibility to take their students beyond word recognition skill development, but frequently they find themselves frustrated because of the shortage of teaching ideas. In short, teachers know the necessity for helping children develop these skills, but find reading program material lacking in this area, either in quantity of teaching ideas or in the sporadic treatment of them. This chapter will provide you with practical yet interesting activities so you will be able to treat these important topics adequately in your instructional program. Your students will go beyond acquisition of word recognition and literal interpretation skills and develop the higher reading skills necessary for fully functioning readers.

	TITLE:	PICK A NUMBER (1)
	PURPOSE:	Understanding sequence.
	ACTIVITY:	Game for two players.
	MATERIALS:	Number board.
	PROCEDURE:	The teacher or a student reads a short story. The child studies the sentences on the board or experience chart. Cover the board. The child must arrange the story in the correct sequence. His partner may ask questions to guide him. For example: What is the title? Answer—#5. What color is the mouse? Answer—#9. What sentence do you select for answer #9?—sentence 1.

MY MOUSE

My mouse is white. My mouse is frisky. Her name is Jeckel. She likes to get out of her cage. The cat chases her. She hides under the bed. Mother puts the cat outside. I catch Jeckel and put her back in the cage.

ILLUSTRATION:

1. The cat chases the mouse	2. Mother puts the cat out	3. She gets out of her cage
4. She is frisky	5. My Mouse	6. I put her back in the cage
7. Her name is Jeckel	8. She hides under the bed	9. My mouse is white

	TITLE:	LUCKY 12 RUMMY (2)
	PURPOSE:	To develop skill in determining sequence.
	ACTIVITY:	Game.
	PROCEDURE:	Have one deck of cards with 48 cards in it. This will include four separate stories, printed in four colors, with 12 sentences in that color. You shuffle the cards and deal five to each player. The player can either draw from the other players (only one card per turn) or from the pile. The object is to get a story in logical order first, with cards whose face sentences are the same color. Skills emphasized: sequence of events.

| | TITLE: | THE TRAIN   (3) |
| | PURPOSE: | Students will be able to show the sequence of the story by putting cards in the correct position in the train. |

ACTIVITY: Game.

MATERIALS: Construction paper, poster board cut into shape of train engine, caboose, cars.

PROCEDURE: Have the students read a certain story. After completion, they will put the order of sequence in each car from engine to caboose.

Each car has a slit in it so that a card can be put into it. The card (cut from construction paper) has a part of the story written on it. The student will put the cards in order of occurrence by placing them in the proper slot on the train.

The cards with details on them should be placed in order from engine, to cars, to caboose.

Example: Our basketball team
was jubilant
with anticipation
of victory

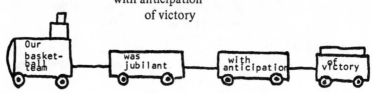

TITLE: PUTTING THE STORY TOGETHER   (4)

PURPOSE: Teaching sequence.

ACTIVITY: Group.

PROCEDURE: Divide a story into ten or 12 parts, pasting them on cards, several paragraphs to a card. Let the children all sit together at the library table with the pack of cards. The object is to read them and put them together in the proper order to have the story make sense.

TITLE: WHAT HAPPENED BEFORE AND AFTER   (5)

PURPOSE: To teach story sequence.

ACTIVITY: Group.

MATERIALS: Library book.

PROCEDURE: The child brings the book to class. When his turn to give a report comes, he designates the page he will read to the class. After the reading, the children ask him questions which bring out what happened before and after the incident read.

TITLE: WRITE THE STORY RIGHT   (6)

PURPOSE: To increase the student's ability to organize ideas from his reading.

ACTIVITY: Game.

MATERIALS: Approximately nine sets of sentences are needed. Each set will contain three or four sentences and will describe a sequence of events. The order of the sentences is scrambled. Each set of scrambled sentences should be written beforehand on paper or poster board large enough for the class to see. Also, each sentence is assigned a letter—a, b, or c.

PROCEDURE: The teacher tells the class they are going to play a game to see which team can unscramble the "story" first. She tells them that after she shows them a set of sentences, which in their correct order tell a story, they are to read the sentences, and then write down the letters assigned to each sentence in the unscrambled order. For example, if the sentences are already in correct order, they would write down a, b, c, d.

She divides the class into three or four teams and repeats that the team whose member at the blackboard unscrambles the sentences first, wins a point for his team. Also, the students not at the board may see if they can unscramble the sentences faster than their teammates at the board.

Example: a. Something more gruesome, though, was grinning at them through the door of the first house.

b. Billy had finished painting his face, and was ready to go trick or treating.

c. That Halloween, their first house was also their last house!

d. He and his friend Mike made a gruesome pair as they approached the first house.

Unscrambled order—b, d, a, c.

TITLE: WHAT'S THE SEQUENCE?   (7)

PURPOSE: To establish the basis for understanding the process of forming sequence.

ACTIVITY: Group.

PROCEDURE: Explain what a sequence actually is with a variety of

187

examples, to determine if the students have grasped the concept.

ILLUSTRATION:

```
┌─────────────────────────────────────────────────┐
│              COMPLETE THESE ORDERS                │
│                                                   │
│   O + O +              _____            │
│                                                   │
│   ☺ ☹ ☺ ☹              _____            │
│                                                   │
│   b d  b d  b d        _____            │
│                                                   │
│   Ooo Ooo              _____            │
│                                                   │
│   △△ O △ △             _____            │
│                                                   │
│   4 8 4 8 4            _____            │
│                                                   │
│                                                   │
│  NAME_____ DATE_____        │
│                                                   │
└─────────────────────────────────────────────────┘
```

TITLE: CARD SEQUENCE   (8)

PURPOSE: The student will illustrate the correct sequence of a story by arranging sentence cards in order.

ACTIVITY: Group.

MATERIALS: Cards on which story events are written—at least two sets.

PROCEDURE: Each group is given a complete set of cards to arrange in correct sequence. The first group to arrange the cards correctly wins.

ILLUSTRATION:

| ANN WENT TO SCHOOL |

| ANN MET JEAN |

| JEAN AND ANN ATE LUNCH |

| JEAN INVITED ANN TO HER HOUSE |

188

TITLE: FOLK TALE (9)

PURPOSE: To aid the child in understanding sequence of events in a story.

ACTIVITY: Group.

MATERIALS: Flannel Board and figures for *Three Little Bears and Goldilocks*. (Any popular folk tale could be used.)

PROCEDURE: Tell the story just as dramatically as possible, illustrating it on your flannel board and particularly emphasizing each new event as it occurs. After telling the story, you might ask the children, "When did the action in the story first start to take place?" As the following events are mentioned, illustrate each of these scenes in proper sequence.

1. The bears starting out for a walk.

2. Goldilocks arriving at the bear's cottage.

3. Goldilocks and the porridge, the chairs, and the beds.

4. Goldilocks being found by the three little bears.

In using a popular folk tale, the child can relive a common experience, readily seeing the main events of the story. From this experience, children could be led to discovering the sequence of events in other stories in their text.

TITLE: SCRAMBLED EGGS (10)

PURPOSE: An exercise to facilitate understanding of sequence.

ACTIVITY: Independent.

MATERIALS: Writing paper and pencils.

PROCEDURE: Write a list of scrambled sentences on the board, explaining that the sentences are mixed up just like scrambled eggs (everyone knows what they are). The word that should come first in the straightened-out sentences will be underlined. The class is to straighten all of the sentences out to make complete thoughts. Work the first sentence with the students, and then let them proceed on their own. Give them a time limit suitable for the individual class or group.

Example: 1. dog has *Jane* new a.

2. raining *Today* is it.

3. after cat bird the ran *The*.

TITLE: UNDERSTANDING SEQUENCE   (11)

PURPOSE: To provide practice in recognition of story sequence.

ACTIVITY: Independent.

MATERIALS: Envelopes, squares of cut paper, a single sentence.

PROCEDURE: Cut short stories into single sentences, numbering each on the back in proper sequence. Put each story into an envelope. Write the following instructions on the outside of each envelope.

> These sentences are mixed up. Arrange them in the proper order to make a story. When you have finished, turn the sentences over, keeping them in the same order. On the back, you will find the numbers 1, 2, 3, 4, 5, etc. If they are in proper order, the sentence is arranged correctly.

Example: These words are mixed up. Arrange them in the proper order to make a complete thought.

> Mama bear, a time, and Baby bear, there were three bears, once upon, Papa bear.

> Once upon a time, there were three bears: Papa bear, Mama bear, and Baby bear.

TITLE: SCRAMBLED COMICS   (12)

PURPOSE: The primary purpose is to develop understanding of sequence of events or logical order. A secondary purpose is to foster creativity.

ACTIVITY: Independent or small group.

MATERIALS: Comic strips that show clearly a sequential order of events, glue, paper, and pencils.

PROCEDURE: 1. Each student or small group is given one scrambled comic (cut out with frames out of order).

2. They are to rearrange it in correct order and explain in sentence form the depicted action.

3. Students then rewrite sentences in paragraph form to relate story action using direct dialogue, if possible.

4. Results are mounted on the bulletin board for all to enjoy.

TITLE:	RECONSTRUCTING THE BIOGRAPHY OF AN AU-THOR (13)
PURPOSE:	To develop the importance of sequence in reading and writing.
ACTIVITY:	Group work. Each student, however, must hand in a paper.
MATERIALS:	Twenty-five cards with idea and fact fragments, paper and pencil.
PROCEDURE:	1. The teacher locates a biography of a writer or poet, etc. (English). It should contain enough information so that 25 ideas or fact cards can be used. *Example*–birth, death, marriage, works, etc. The teacher then makes 25 cards.
	2. After the cards are made, they are shuffled and arranged in five groups of five cards each.
	3. Groups are formed. Each group should have one good academic leader and each group receives one set of five cards.
	4. Groups then work on facts, creating sentences and developing some kind of brief. Each student makes his own copy.
	5. Facts are then exchanged and new facts are joined with others.
	6. After all facts have been exchanged, a complete biography is turned in by each student.
	7. Each group should differ, but within the group the biographies should be the same.
	8. Mimeographs are made of each group's biographies and analyzed for logical sequence and development.

ILLUSTRATION:

Born: April 12, 1873	Poet is: Robert Frost
Delivered speech Kennedy Inauguration	"Death of Hired Man" One of most famous

TITLE:	LET'S BE A MONTH FINDER (14)
PURPOSE:	To provide practice in reading the months of the year and reading clues to each month. To teach the sequence of the months.
ACTIVITY:	Group.
MATERIALS:	Tagboard strips (backed with sandpaper) on which clues of

the months are written in bold print. Tagboard strips (backed with sandpaper) on which the names of the months are written. Flannel board.

PROCEDURE: Each child is given a strip with a clue and a month (randomly). Decide, with the children, which clue comes first and have the child with that clue place it on the flannel board. The child who has January places the month alongside of the clue. Continue until all months and clues are on the flannel board in sequential order. When completed, the children can reread the clues and months. This will reinforce the sequence of the months.

Example:
1. The month that starts the year. (January)
2. The month we have Valentine's Day. (February)
3. The month that Spring begins. (March)
4. The month that has a Fool's Day. (April)
5. The month we have Mother's Day. (May)
6. The month that school is out. (June)
7. The month we celebrate Independence Day. (July)
8. The month of the year that summer ends. (August)
9. The month that school starts. (September)
10. The month we have Halloween. (October)
11. The month we have Thanksgiving Day. (November)
12. The month we have Christmas. (December)

TITLE: WHICH WAY?   (15)

PURPOSE: To develop the ability to tell a story in proper sequence.

ACTIVITY: Independent or small group.

MATERIALS: Four or five story pictures pasted on individual pieces of cardboard.

PROCEDURE: The child places the group of story pictures on his desk. He then arranges them in the proper sequence to depict the story in its logical order. When completed and checked by the teacher, he may tell his story to a small group of children and then return it to the box.

ILLUSTRATION:

2	1	3
Cow jumping over the moon	Cat playing the fiddle	dog laughing to see such sport

TITLE: RIDDLES (16)

PURPOSE: To develop the habit of reading carefully so that thoughtful conclusions can be reached.

ACTIVITY: Game.

PROCEDURE: Make up a number of riddles written on cards. Each player takes a card and tries to guess the riddle. The child who guesses the most riddles is the winner. (The sentence should be specific enough to aid children in guessing the riddle. The answer to the riddle should be written on the back of the card so that it can be checked.)

ILLUSTRATION:

> I AM A PLACE IN A CITY. ELEPHANTS, BEARS, MONKEYS, AND KANGAROOS LIVE IN ME. MEN TAKE CARE OF THE ANIMALS. CHILDREN LIKE TO VISIT ME. WHAT AM I?
>
> (Zoo)

> I AM HARD. PEOPLE WALK ON ME. SOMETIMES I AM MADE OF PRETTY COLORS. A MOP IS USED TO KEEP ME CLEAN. WHAT AM I?
>
> (Floor)

TITLE: WHAT IS IT? (17)

PURPOSE: The student will *formulate conclusions* by solving a verbal puzzle.

ACTIVITY: Game.

PROCEDURE: The teacher stands in front of the room. The children are seated. She starts out with, "I am thinking of something big. It has hair all over its body and can walk on two legs or four legs. It growls. It can swing on a vine. It lives in Africa. What is it?"

The first child to guess the answer then gets a chance to stand up and give a verbal puzzle.

TITLE: TWENTY QUESTIONS (18)

PURPOSE: Formulating conclusions.

193

ACTIVITY: Game.

PROCEDURE: One student or team chooses a date, person, place, period, or event which the class has studied. He (or they) may be asked 20 questions to which he may answer only Yes or No.

Example: Is it a place? No.
Is it a person? Yes.
Is it a man? Yes.
Is he still living? No.
Is he from American History? Yes.
Is he from the Industrial Revolution? No.
Is he from the Colonial Period? Yes.
Was he a statesman? Yes.
The first President? No.
The third President? Yes.
Thomas Jefferson? Yes.

TITLE: STAND UP AND BE MEASURED   (19)

PURPOSE: The students will learn how to form conclusions based on information about themselves.

ACTIVITY: Group.

MATERIALS: Poster board, large.
Ruler.
Colored crayons (or pencils).
Measuring tape.

PROCEDURE: Children will be measured for their accurate height. They will be responsible for writing it down until they are called upon to be measured. A chart will be made using a scale of 1 inch for 1 inch of height. This will be put vertically on the chart. The students' names will be written (by them) alphabetically along the bottom edge of the chart. One by one, they will color their height in the specified column. When the activity is completed, observations can be made as to where they stand in relation to the rest of the class. (*Example:* 70% are shorter than me.)

ILLUSTRATION:

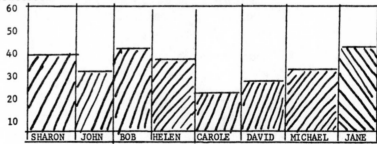

194

TITLE: HOW WILL THE STORY END? (20)

PURPOSE: To help children formulate conclusions.

ACTIVITY: Group.

MATERIALS: Textbooks.

PROCEDURE: Have the class read at least half of a story and then close their books. Giving careful consideration to the events and circumstances, the children must try to figure out what the outcome of the story will be. Various members of the class should have a chance to tell what they think constitutes a good ending and why. Next, have the class finish reading the story and see whether or not they formed the right conclusions. This exercise can best be done with stories about historical events or parts of chapters in a science book.

TITLE: THE FOX AND THE STORK (21)

PURPOSE: The student will discuss a stated opinion for validity and draw conclusions based on past experience.

ACTIVITY: Group (small).

MATERIALS: Printed copies of a short reading or selection that clearly states an opinion, with pertinent, thought-provoking questions.

PROCEDURE: Either read the selection orally or have the students read it silently. Questions should be discussed in the group; conclusions may be recorded.

ILLUSTRATION: "The Fox and the Stork"

At one time the Fox and the Stork were on visiting terms and seemed very good friends. So the Fox invited the Stork to dinner and for a joke put nothing before her but some soup in a very shallow dish. This the Fox could easily lap up, but the Stork could only wet the end of her long bill in it and left the meal as hungry as when she began.

"I am sorry," said the Fox, "the soup is not to your liking." "Pray do not apologize," said the Stork. "I hope you will return this visit, and come and dine with me soon."

So a day was appointed when the Fox should visit the Stork, but when they were seated at the table, all there was for their dinner was contained in a very long-necked jar with a narrow mouth, in which the Fox could not insert his snout, so all he could manage to do was to lick the outside of the jar.

"I will not apologize for the dinner," said the Stork:

"One bad turn deserves another."

Aesop

Questions: 1. Do you think the Fox and the Stork were ever good friends?
2. This story was written to illustrate a moral. What is the moral? Do you agree with it?
3. Can you think of another way the stork might have acted?
4. Can you think of other morals expressing opposite viewpoints?
5. From reading this, what kind of person do you think Aesop was? Could he have been teasing us, by making us think he lives by this moral?
6. What do you think would happen if you lived by this moral?

TITLE: **VALIDITY**   (22)

PURPOSE: Provide practice in distinguishing valid and invalid conclusions, formulated from a given story.

ACTIVITY: Group.

PROCEDURE: The teacher formulates valid as well as invalid conclusions pertaining to a given story. Each conclusion should be written on a 2" x 4" card, assigning a number from 1 to 8 to each card. Cards such as the following should be made for each child.

After reading the story to the group, the teacher randomly draws cards with conclusions, reading the statement and the number code. The children should mark the number under the proper column, indicating a valid or invalid conclusion. The first child to mark all eight valid statements is the winner.

ILLUSTRATION:

Valid	Invalid
1	1
2	2
3	3
4	4

Valid	Invalid
5	5
6	6
7	7
8	8

TITLE: WHO AM I?   (23)

PURPOSE: To provide practice in thinking and drawing conclusions.

ACTIVITY: Independent.

MATERIALS: Mimeographed work on paper.

PROCEDURE: Read each paragraph and use the facts in it to decide who each person is. Then draw a line under the worker who is talking.

> *Example:* My first chore is to check all the boxes, jars, and cans in my cupboards. Next, I grease my pans and pie tins. Then I collect the eggs, milk, flour, salt, and anything else I need before mixing pies and cakes. Later I boil sugar, melted butter, and vegetable coloring to make pretty decorations.
>
> Chemist   *Baker*
> Milkman   Tailor

TITLE: FILL IN THE STORY   (24)

PURPOSE: Following directions and formulating conclusions.

MATERIALS: Poster paper on which the opening scene of a story has been represented by the use of illustrations.

ACTIVITY: Independent.

PROCEDURE: The students will bring in various pictures of a topic of general interest and construct a poster dealing with the main topic of the story. After a brief introduction, ask them to write the conclusion of the story.

> *Example:* A poster has been completed which deals with witch trials. The students have discussed various techniques and devices used to seek out witches. Introduce a story about a witch (originality is the key) and ask the students to complete the story. Then allow students to compare their ideas and have copies made to share with the class.

197

TITLE: WHAT WILL HAPPEN? (25)

PURPOSE: To develop the ability to predict a conclusion or outcome.

MATERIALS: Eight and a half by eleven cardboard with two or three pictures pasted on it; baggy plastic bag stapled on the back of the cardboard for the rest of the pieces to the pictures.

PROCEDURE: The child puts the pieces from the bag on his desk beside the cardboard. He looks at the pasted pictures and determines which piece will depict the outcome of the story picture on the cardboard. After the teacher checks his card, he returns it to the box.

ILLUSTRATION:

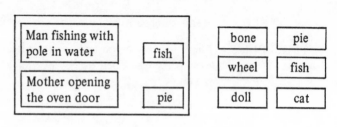

TITLE: CUBE SENTENCE (26)

PURPOSE: To help students create sentences using blocks.

PLAYERS: One to four.

ACTIVITY: Game.

PROCEDURE: Cube Sentence is similar to Word Puzzle, but the child makes sentences with cubes which have words on all four sides.

ILLUSTRATION:

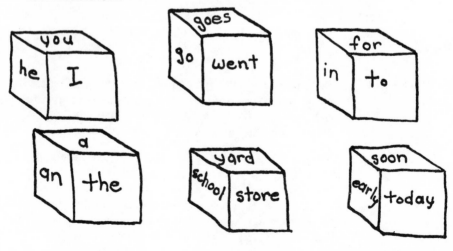

198

TITLE:	SENTENCE PUZZLE	(27)

PURPOSE: To arrange words to make sentences and correctly fit the puzzle.

PLAYERS: One to four.

PROCEDURE: The child has a set of words on separate pieces of puzzle. Each group of words are different colors designating the different parts of a sentence: subject, verb, and direct object. The pieces are in the form of a puzzle. In order for the sentence to be correct, the pieces have to fit.

This game can be used to reinforce or review words, introduce new words, or simply as an educational game for fun.

ILLUSTRATION:

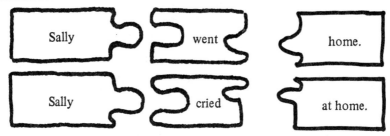

TITLE:	ACTION SENTENCES	(28)

PURPOSE: To introduce the concept of combining familiar words to construct complete thoughts.

ACTIVITY: Game involving as many as the entire class.

MATERIALS: Five- by eight-inch index cards, tape.

PROCEDURE: The teacher distributes a 5" x 8" index card with a basic familiar noun, verb, or adjective printed large on it to each child. The children then tape the cards to their clothing and move freely about the room to find other words with which to form a sentence. They are allowed two to five minutes and then sit down by their other sentence members. One group at a time stands and presents their sentence to the class.

ILLUSTRATION:

TITLE: MIXUPS AND FIXUPS   (29)

PURPOSE: The purpose of this activity is to give students practice in building sentences and reading them fluently and meaningfully.

ACTIVITY: Group game.

MATERIALS: Forty cards are used. On each of the cards there is written half of one of the 20 broken-up sentences. Each sentence is broken into its subject and predicate, one on each card. Each subject card forms a meaningful sentence only when combined with its own predicate card.

PROCEDURE: All cards are shuffled and placed face down in the chalk shelf. The teacher calls on various children to take turns turning up the top card, reading it aloud, and putting it to the left in the pocket chart if it is a subject card, to the right if it is a predicate card. The children should read the resulting nonsense sentence. The players take turns following the above procedure. When one card forms a meaningful sentence with another that has already been turned up, the player reads the complete sentence and takes both cards as his trick. The player with the greater number of tricks wins.

Each time, when he takes a card and is looking for the proper complement, the player should be allowed to read a nonsense sentence aloud, such as, "A hen drives the truck," "Mom is in the crib," etc.

Example: Possible sentences include the following:

Subject Card	*Predicate Card*
1. The ship	has a mast
2. The doll	is in the crib.
3. A hen	has wings.
4. The dress	hangs on the rack.
5. The clock	says tick-tock.
6. Mom	mends a sock.
7. A man	drives a truck.
8. The tree	is full of buds.
9. The bulb	is in the lamp.

TITLE: SENTENCE SCRABBLE   (30)

PURPOSE: To help build skills in sentence building.

ACTIVITY: Game.

200

MATERIALS: A playing board laid out similar to a Scrabble board, except that "double letter," etc., would be replaced by "double word," and "double word" would be replaced by "double sentence."

Cards the same size as the squares on the board, with common and difficult words written on each card. Each card should also have a small number written on it for the value of the card, the value based on the difficulty of being able to use the word in a sentence. Blank cards may be used which would have no value and could be used for any word.

A type of stand, like in Scrabble, which would hold the cards, with the other players seeing the cards.

PROCEDURE: The game is played like Scrabble except that sentences instead of words are built.

ILLUSTRATION:

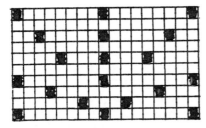 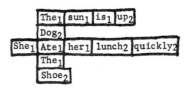

TITLE: SENTENCE BUILDING VIA FLANNEL BOARD (31)

PURPOSE: To reinforce sentence structure.

ACTIVITY: Game.

MATERIALS: Cardboard strips (made from cardboard, stockings, or construction paper). A small flannel board.

PROCEDURE: Choose several four- or five-word sentences and select a group of children or a committee to print each word on a cardboard strip. Scramble the words on the flannel board; let each child write them in good sentence form. Then let him arrange the words correctly on the flannel board.

ILLUSTRATION:

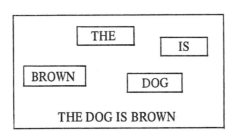

TITLE: JUMBLED SENTENCES   (32)

PURPOSE: To give students practice in making sensible sentences.

ACTIVITY: Group.

PROCEDURE: Give the following directions once—rearrange the words in the sentence to make sense, and on the line next to the sentence, tell whether the sentence is true or false. Make these up on ditto sheets.

1. For gasoline use fuel autos.
2. Winter is New York in cold.
3. Trees on grow oak apples.
4. Dog a insect is an.
5. Temperature be zero below may in the January.

TITLE: SCRAMBLED WORDS   (33)

PURPOSE: Putting groups of words into an order which communicates will help students develop sentence sense.

ACTIVITY: Group or independent.

PROCEDURE: Give the pupils much practice in putting groups of words into an order which communicates. This can be done as a writing exercise in which scrambled words are given for the pupil to make into a sentence. The teacher can: (1) prepare this exercise on a ditto, or (2) give each child a large piece of cardboard with a word printed on it and have the pupils stand in front of the room holding their cards. They must then shift their positions to get the words into an order which communicates a message.

Example: with a fluffy was a bunny There once white tail. (There once was a bunny with a fluffy white tail.)

TITLE: BUILD A SENTENCE   (34)

PURPOSE: Improvement of phrasing.

ACTIVITY: Group.

MATERIALS: Strips of cardboard approximately 4 inches wide and 24 inches long. Take a story or make one up and divide it into phrases, printing a phrase on each strip. Then make other strips with phrases from another story and do the same thing.

You could have a story that reads:

Once upon a time
    a little boy
        lived in a big house.

He lived
    with his mother
        and his father.

He lived
    with his sister
        and three brothers.

As you can see, most of the story parts can be interchanged but would have to be in proper order to make sense. Also, little boys do not live in tall trees.

PROCEDURE: The teacher can choose a beginning phrase and have the child holding that phrase (all the cards are passed out to children in the group) come to the front of the room and stand facing the other children. Then another child could add to the sentence, and so on until a complete sentence is facing the children. After the sentence is completed, the teacher could ask someone to read the sentence aloud.

Note: Individual words can be used in this same manner to make sentences and would help children improve their word recognition.

ILLUSTRATION:

TITLE: PUMPKIN ROOT   (35)

PURPOSE: Word building (or sentence building).

ACTIVITY: Group.

PROCEDURE: Using many small cards, write one word containing a prefix or a suffix on each. You may use some more than once. Put word cards in a plastic pumpkin in the classroom. At certain times during each day of Halloween week, let each child draw a word out of the pumpkin. If he can name the root word (or make a correct sentence using the word), he may keep the card. The one with the most cards at the end of the week is the winner.

This can also be played with a few students drawing cards out (in turn) at one time.

TITLE: DIAL-A-WORD   (36)

PURPOSE: To help students develop vocabulary and sentence structure.

ACTIVITY: Group.

MATERIALS: A large wheel constructed in the manner illustrated.

a—solid color paper.
b—open space where word shows through.
c—fastener to make wheel pin.
d—a piece of paper is behind "a" that the words are written on.

PROCEDURE: The teacher or a student spins the wheel to land on a word. With the word, the students make sentences, define, or engage in various activities that are explained below.

Variations—(a) Orally make sentences.
           (b) Written tests.
           (c) Can insert different words as the students progress.
           (d) Dictionary study.
           (e) Can use the wheel for special help.
           (f) Pronunciation help.

Types of words used could be taken from spelling lists of many different grades. For the lower grades, letters could be used to help with spelling or reading.

Students could help make the wheel and use words that they know so that they could get started with some success.

Make the Dial-a-Word Wheel as colorful and unique as possible to stimulate interest and a desire to work, and use the wheel to help them learn.

ILLUSTRATION:

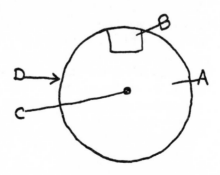

TITLE: SENTENCES FOR HALLOWEEN   (37)

PURPOSE: To acquaint students with the technique of creative writing through the use of key words.

ACTIVITY: Group or independent.

MATERIALS: Pencil and paper, mounting paper.

PROCEDURE: A topic is selected for the writing assignment and written on the blackboard, accompanied by the appropriate key words. Each student is to use the key words plus any verbs necessary to create a meaningful paragraph. The pupil whose story is worthy of recognition (as proved through his use of the key words) has the work mounted, then posted on the bulletin board.

Example: Topic–Halloween
Key Words–Halloween, witch, goblin, ghost, owl, broom, cat, trick-or-treat(ers), boo, black, night, trees, moon.

It was Halloween night. An owl was hooting, the trees were shaking, the wind was blowing, and the moon shone above. Across the moon's surface, a witch was flying on her broom with a black cat at her side. The goblins were out and so were the ghosts, who were frightening trick-or-treaters by shouting "boo!"

TITLE: THE HARD AND SOFT SOUNDS OF "G"   (38)

PURPOSE: To provide practice in sentence building and continuity of thought in paragraph building.

ACTIVITY: Small group (not more than eight).

MATERIALS: Ditto sheets containing word lists and instructions to place an *H* or *S* in the blank space before each word containing a hard or soft *g*. Tape recorder for use after completion of paper work.

PROCEDURE: Students work independently to identify the sounds of G. After completing the paper work, they will make sentences orally, using each word either in a single sentence or several words in one sentence. After one or two tries, they will then attempt to create sentences related to the previous sentence. The third time around, they will create sentences in sequence to form a paragraph. The student appointed as scribe (or teacher) will write down sentences as they are verbalized, and when a sequential paragraph is completed, students read what they have written. The best oral reader in the group will record the paragraph on tape.

garden	grandma	hungry	wagon
magic	rug	frog	hedge
village	orange	graveyard	

TITLE: MOOD BINGO (39)

PURPOSE: To interpret mood and feeling through words and oral reading by choosing the correct word to be marked on the bingo card.

ACTIVITY: Group.

PROCEDURE: Each player is given a bingo card and markers. The caller instructs the players to pick the word that best describes the mood or feeling of a passage that is read aloud. The caller will call out the number of the passage and the player must write the correct number on the marker and place it on the word on the bingo card.

Variations: This can be played using all synonyms or antonyms. The caller would call out a word and the student would place a marker on the word with the similar meaning, or if playing with antonyms, he would mark the word with the opposite meaning.

ILLUSTRATION: Use the standard bingo cards with words written in the squares.

B	I	N	G	O
eager	amazed	surprised	frightened	unhappy
stern	contented	terrified	scornful	worried
sad	excited	FREE	doubtful	silly
guilty	proud	annoyed	disgusted	sad
afraid	happy	dismayed	wondering	scornful

TITLE: CREATING STUDENT PLAYS (40)

PURPOSE: To develop fluent oral reading.

ACTIVITY: Group.

MATERIALS: Select or write (depending on how creative you are or your children are) enough plays for each of your groups in your classroom. The plays should be at the students' general reading level or one level below for total enjoyment and pleasure.

PROCEDURE: Day 1—Issue plays and have students read the different parts. Let each student practice his or her part and stress the use of expression when reading orally.

Day 2—Each group presents their play—*reading* their parts, not memorizing them.

TITLE: IMPROVING ORAL INTERPRETATION   (41)

PURPOSE: To practice reading with expression.

ACTIVITY: Group.

PROCEDURE: Write several declarative, exclamatory, and interrogative sentences on slips of paper and put them in a box in front of the room. Make three cards for each child in the class. On one card put a period, on another put a question mark, and on the other put an exclamation mark.

Divide the class into two teams. Pass out the cards to the children, making sure each child has all three cards. Then have a child from Team A come up to the front of the room and select a slip of paper from the box. The child reads the sentence on his slip of paper to the class with expression so that the class will know what type of sentence he is reading. After the child has read his sentence to the class, the students hold up the card that has the end punctuation mark for the sentence the child read. The teacher or a scorekeeper counts the students in Team A and in Team B who answered correctly and records that number on the board for each team. Then a child from Team B goes to the front of the room and the same procedure is followed. After each child has had a turn, the points are tallied and the winning team gets something special.

TITLE: INDEPENDENT READING   (42)

PURPOSE: To build skill in oral reading.

ACTIVITY: Independent.

MATERIALS: Slides of a story, with one paragraph per slide.
A cassette taping of the story with a "beep" and pause between the paragraphs corresponding with the slides.
A blank cassette.
A cassette-type recorder-player.

A slide viewer where one person looks at one slide at a time.

PROCEDURE: The student reads the story silently while listening to the recording of the story. This will help him hear how it should sound and learn unknown words. It should also improve his silent reading skills. He may need to do this more than once per story. Slides are changed at "beep."

After hearing the story, the child records his oral reading of the story. This will give both the student and the teacher an opportunity to evaluate his work.

10

Treasures for Reading Teachers from Commercial Sources

• • • • • • • • • • • • •

This chapter is different from the others. Whereas preceding chapters reveal creative teaching ideas, this one contains commercial sources for easy-reading book series, multi-level instructional materials to meet individual needs, reading games and activities, and publishers' addresses, to give you a materials source from which to draw upon.

To have a viable reading program, a teacher needs many materials available. Consequently, creative teachers are constantly searching for additional reading materials to purchase when funds become available. The materials listed in this chapter are a resource, to be used whenever there is a possibility of acquiring reading materials.

In the first section of this chapter, you will find easily read book series with their readability levels, making it convenient for you to look down the readability column for particular levels of difficulty. In another column is the publisher's number, and with this number you can quickly locate the publisher's address on the last few pages of this chapter.

The second part of this chapter is Section B, containing instructional materials other than books. These rich materials are valuable assets in meeting the multi-level reading needs of your students. Again, the level is provided along with the publisher's number.

Any exciting reading program probably contains games, for games induce interest and excitement. Section C provides you with a healthy list of games you may select from to meet the instructional needs of your students. Opposite each game is the estimated level for your information; however, keep in mind that any reading material is usable with students at any grade level if the students' reading levels coincide with the material difficulty level.

All in all, Chapter 10 is a reference source to help you locate commercial reading materials appropriate for your needs.

PART II

A. Easily read books for reading instruction.

Teachers at all grade levels need a wide variety of reading materials. Following is a list of book series with their readability levels which are recommended for independent reading and for instructional purposes. Readability levels are estimated utilizing vocabulary level, sentence length, and experience in using the book with children whose reading level is known. The coding is:

R—readiness, PP—pre-primer, P—primer, 1—first reading level, and so on. PP-4 stands for readability pre-primer through fourth reading level.

To save space, each publisher is numbered. The list of publishers may be found at the end of this chapter for easy reference.

Name of Series	Readability Level	Publisher Number
American Reading Round Table	PP-4	2
See and Say	R	2
Adventure	3-4	9
Butternut Bill	PP-P	9
Buttons Family Adventure	PP-3	9
Cowboy Sam	PP-3	9
Dan Frontier	PP-4	9
Easy to Read Books	PP	9
Invitation to Adventure	PP-2	9
Jerry	PP-3	9
Moonbeam	PP-1	9
Sailor Jack	PP-3	9
Space Travel Books	1-3	9
Tom Logan	PP-2	9
Tommy O'Toole	1-3	9
World of Adventure	2-6	9
Childhood of Famous Americans	3	11
Folk Tales Around the World	4-6	11
Frontiers of America	4	16
I Want to Be	2	16
We Live in the City	1	16
The Tizz Books	2	16
Presidents, Pitchers and Passers	4-6	16

Name of Series	Readability Level	Publisher Number
Yearling Books	2-6	20
Signal Books	1-4	22
Martin Moonay's Minute Mysteries	4-6	27
Just Beginning to Read	PP	31
Beginning to Read Books	1-2	31
Interesting Reading Series	2-3	31
Basic Vocabulary Series	2	33
Discovery Books	2	33
First Books	1	33
Folklore Books	3	33
Pleasure Reading Series	3	33
Reading Shelf	1-3	33
Indians	3	33
Scouting	3	33
Holidays	3	33
Sports	4	33
Modern Literature	6	35
Adapted Classics	3-5	35
An Early-Start Reader	R	37
Easy Reader Books	2	37
Signature Books	6	37
We Were There Books	6	37
Young Readers' Bookshelf	6	37
Adventure in Space	6	37
All About Books	4-6	39
Beginner Books	1-2	39
Easy to Read Books	3	39
Easy to Read Science Library	3	39
Landmark Books	5-6	39
American Adventure	2-6	43
Checkered Flag	2	44
Deep Sea Adventures	2-5	44
Jim Forest	2-3	44
Morgan Bay Mysteries	3-4	44
Reading Motivated	4	44
The Time Machine	PP-3	44
Wildlife Adventure	4-5	44
Our Animal Story Books	1	46
Walt Disney Story Books	1-2	46

Name of Series	Readability Level	Publisher Number
Teen-Age Tales	5-6	46
It's Fun to Find Out Story Books	3-4	46
My Schoolbook of Picture Stories	R-1	47
Working Wheels	R-1	47
Easy to Read Series	2	48
Piper Books	4	48
North Star Books	5-6	48
Aviation Readers	P-3	57
Macmillan Readers Unit Books	PP-3	57
Sports Readers	2-3	57
Horse in No Hurry	3	76
Step-Up Books	2	77
Pegasus Story Books	2-3	78
Famous Story	6	81
Sanborn Readers	P-3	81
Special Reading Books	3-6	84
Reading for Independence	2-3	84
Social Learning Readers	1-3	85
Easy Readers	PP-4	86
Little League Books	5-6	86
Treasure Books	5-6	86
Navajo	3-5	92
Pueblo	3-5	92
Everyday Readers	4	95
Junior Everyreader	3-4	95

B. Other Instructional Materials to Meet Multi-Level Reading Needs

A wide variety of instructional materials is essential to assist children in improving their reading. Following are materials which are useful in this process, with the reading level indicated. You should keep in mind that pupils with reading abilities above these levels can frequently profit from using these materials to correct specific reading difficulties.

Materials	Level	Publisher Number
Weekly Reader Practice Books	Primary-6	4
Independent Activities	1-2	4

Materials	Level	Publisher Number
Creative Expression Series	3-4	4
Working with Sounds Books A-D	1-4	8
Using the Context Books A-F	1-6	8
Locating the Answer Books B-D	2-4	8
Following Directions Books A-D	1-4	8
Getting the Facts Books C-E	3-5	8
Developmental Reading Series	Primer-6	11
Reading Readiness Series	K-1	18
Reading Thinking Skills	Primer-6	18
Steps to Mastery of Words	1-6	25
Magic Squares Game Book	4-6	27
Sounds We Use Book I	1	31
Readiness for Reading	Primary	33
Happy Bears Reading Set	Pre-Primer	33
My Puzzle Book 1 and 2	Primary	33
Sounds We Use	Primary	34
Creative Thinking Materials	1-8	34
Silent Readers with Comprehension Tests	5	40
Phonogram Books 1-4	Primary	41
Speech to Print Phonics	Primary	42
Study Exercises for Developing Reading Skills Series	4-6	53
Seatwork for Reading with Phonics	Primary	54
My Word Book Series	1-8	56
Phonics We Use	Primer-6	56
Reading and Spectrum of Skills	1-6	57
Building Reading Skills	2-6	58
Puzzle Workbooks	R	58
Diagnostic Reading Workbooks	4-6	61
New Phonics Skilltext Series	R-4	61
Reading Skilltext Series	1-6	61
Be a Better Reader	4-9	74
Reader's Digest Skillbuilders	1-8	78
Read, Learn, Improve	4-6	79
Keyword Puzzle	4-6	79
SRA Reading Laboratories	Primary-H.S.	83
SRA Pilot Libraries	4-9	83

Materials	Level	Publisher Number
SRA Reading for Understanding	3-8	83
Gates-Peardon Reading Exercises	3-8	89
McCall-Crabbs Test Lessons	3-7	89
McCall-Hardy Test Lessons	Primary	89
Read Along with Me Series	Primer	89
Crossword Puzzles	1-6	91
Classroom Reading Clinic #10	1-6	95
Webster Word Wheels	3-6	95
Conquests in Reading	1-6	95
The Magic World of Dr. Spello	1-6	95
New Practice Readers	2-8	95
Practice Readers	3-6	95
Basic Goals in Reading	2-4	95
Phonics Eye and Ear Fun	1-4	95
Using Our Language	4-6	95
Word Analysis Charts	3-6	95

C.   Commercial Reading Games and Activities   *Level*

AMERICANA INTERSTATE CORP. Mundalein, Illinois 60060

    Listen and Learn with Phonics   Primary

APPLETON-CENTURY-CROFTS, 440 Park Avenue South, N.Y., N.Y. 10015

    Language Lotto   Pre-School

DEXTER AND WESTBROOK, Rockville Centre, New York

    We Read Sentences A-1   Primary
    We Read Sentences A-2   Primary
    Pronoun Parade   Intermediate
    Riddle, Riddle Rhyme Time   Primary

EDUCATIONAL STIMULI, 2012 Hammond Avenue, Superior, Wisconsin

    Beano Vocabulary Game   Intermediate

THE GARRARD PRESS, 510 N. Hickory Street, Champaign, Illinois

    Dolch Aids-to-Reading Materials

        Picture Readiness Game   Readiness
        Who Gets It?   Readiness
        Match, Set II   Readiness
        Consonant Cards   Readiness

Vowel Cards	Readiness
Picture Word Cards	Readiness
Popper Words, Set II, Group Size	First
Popper Words, Set 1	First
Popper Words Set 2	Second
Basic Sight Words	Second
Sight Phrase Cards	Third
What the Letters Say	First
Consonant Lotto	First
Vowel Lotto	Second
Take	Third
Syllable Game	Third
Group Sounding Game	Third
Know Your States	Third
Read and Say Verb Game	Third

HARPER AND ROW, INC., 2500 Crawford Avenue, Evanston, Illinois 60201

Word-Go-Round (Teacher's Instructions)	Primary

HOUGHTON MIFFLIN, 1900 S. Batavia Avenue, Geneva, Illinois 60134

Get Set

Broken Letters	Primary
Animal Race	Primary
Pickalift	Primary
Picture Words	Primary
Silly Sentences	Primary
Sentence Train	Primary
Dominoes	Primary
Stop-Dot	Primary

IDEAL SCHOOL SUPPLY COMPANY, 8312-8346 Dirkhoff Ave., Chicago, Illinois 60620

Quiet Pal Game	Primary
The End-in-E Game	Primary
Rhyming Puzzle	Primary
Magic Cards Opposites	Primary
Magic Consonant Blends	Primary
Magic Cards Initial Consonants	Primary
Magic Cards Vowels	Primary

INSTRUCTO CORPORATION, Paoli, Pennsylvania 193-1

Castle Rhyming Picture Game	Primary
Rhyming Card Game	Primary
Pirate Rhyming Picture Game	Primary

THE JUDY COMPANY, 310 North 2nd St., Minneapolis, 1, Minnesota 55401

See-Quees
Humpty Dumpty	Primary
Gingerbread Boy	Primary

KENWORTHY EDUCATIONAL SERVICE, Buffalo, New York

Doghouse Game	Primary
Junior Phonic Rummy	Primary
ABC Game	Primary

LYONS AND CARNAHAN, 407 E. 25th St., Chicago, Illinois 60616

Phonics We Use Learning Games Kit	Primary

MILTON BRADLEY CO., Springfield, Illinois

Phonetic Word Wheel	Primary
Beginning Sounds—Flannel Board	Primary
Sequence Cards	Primary
Sentence Builder	Primary

F. A. OWEN PUBLISHING CO., Dansville, New York 14437

Picture Word Flash Cards	Primary
Vowels and Vowel Digraphs (Charts—Cards)	Primary

PARKER BROTHERS, INC., Salem, Massachusetts

Play'n Talk—Phonics in Action Game	Elementary

PLYMOUTH PRESS, 1232 West 79th Street, Chicago, Illinois 60620

Perfo Seat Work in Silent Reading, Easy Riddles and Other Activities	Primary

SCOTT FORESMAN AND COMPANY, 1900 E. Lake, Glenview, Illinois 60025

Linguistic Block Series

Rolling Phonics—Vowels (Teacher's Guide)	Primary
Rolling Reader (Teacher's Guide)	Second

STECK-VAUGHN CO., Box 16, Austin, Texas 78761

Reading Essentials Teaching Aids	First
Phono-Word Wheels	Primary
Swap	4-8

TEACHER RESOURCES, INC., 334 Boylston St., Boston, Massachusetts 02116

Show You Know—Then Go (Phonics Game)	Primary
See and Say Puzzle Cards	Primary

WEBER-COSTELLO, Chicago, Illinois

Language Arts Activity Cards	Primary

PUBLISHERS' ADDRESSES

1. Allyn and Bacon, 310 W. Polk Street, Chicago, Illinois 60607
2. American Book Company, 55 Fifth Avenue, New York, New York 10003

3. American Council on Education, 1785 Massachusetts Avenue, Washington, D.C. 20036
4. American Education Publications, Education Center, Columbus, Ohio 43216
5. American Textbook Publishers Institute, 432 Park Avenue South, New York, New York 10016
6. Arthur C. Croft Publications, 100 Garfield Avenue, New London, Connecticut 06320
7. Bantam Books, Inc., 271 Madison Avenue, New York, New York 10016
8. Barnell Loft, Ltd., 111 S. Centre Avenue, Rockville Centre, Long Island, New York 11570
9. Benefic Press, 1900 North Narragansett, Chicago, Illinois 60639
10. Berkley Publishing Corporation, 15 E. 26th Street, New York, New York 10010
11. Bobbs-Merrill Company, 4300 W. 62nd Street, Indianapolis, Indiana 46206
12. Wm. Brown Company, Publishers, 135 S. Locust Street, Dubuque, Iowa 52001
13. California Test Bureau, Del Monte Research Park, Monterey, California 33940
14. Campbell and Hall, 1047 Commonwealth Avenue, Boston, Massachusetts 02107
15. Chandler Publishing Company, 124 Spear Street, San Francisco, California 94105
16. Children's Press, Inc., Jackson Boulevard and Racine Avenue, Chicago, Illinois 60607
17. Committee on Diagnostic Reading Tests, Inc., Mountain Home, North Carolina 27801
18. Continental Press, Inc., Elizabethtown, Pennsylvania 17022
19. Dartnell Corporation, Chicago, Illinois 60640
20. Dell Publishing Company, Inc., 750 Third Avenue, New York, New York 10017
21. Direct Approach Methods, Inc., 93 Sherwood, Hambur, New York 14075
22. Doubleday and Company, Inc., Garden City, Long Island, New York 11531
23. Eastern Montana College, Billings, Montana 59101
24. Educational Developmental Laboratories, Huntington, New York 11744
25. Educational Service, Inc., Benton Harbor, Michigan 49022
26. Educational Testing Service, Princeton, New Jersey 08540
27. Educators Publishing Service, Inc., 3rd Vassar Street, Cambridge, Massachusetts 02139
28. Encyclopaedia Britannica Press, 425 N. Michigan Avenue, Chicago, Illinois 60611
29. Expression Company, Magnolia, Massachusetts 01930
30. Fearon Publishers, Palo Alto, California 94306
31. Follett Publishing Company, 1010 W. Washington Boulevard, Chicago, Illinois 60607

32. Fund for Perceptually Handicapped Children, Inc., P.O. Box 656, Evanston, Illinois 60204
33. Garrard Press, 510 N. Hickory Street, Champaign, Illinois 61820
34. Ginn and Company, 450 W. Algonquin Road, Arlington Heights, Illinois 60005
35. Globe Book Company, 175 Fifth Avenue, New York, New York 10010
36. Grolier Society, Inc., 575 Lexington Avenue, New York, New York 10022
37. Grosset and Dunlap, Inc., 51 Madison Avenue, New York, New York 10010
38. Guild Press, Inc., Poughkeepsie, New York 12601
39. E. M. Hale and Company, 1201 S. Hastings Way, Eau Clair, Wisconsin 54702
40. Hall and McCreary Company, Park Avenue at 6th Street, Minneapolis, Minnesota 55415
41. C. S. Hammond and Company, Maplewood, New Jersey 07040
42. Harcourt, Brace & World, Inc., 7555 Caldwell Avenue, Chicago, Illinois 60648
43. Harper and Row Publishers, 2500 Crawford Avenue, Evanston, Illinois 60201
44. Harr-Wagner Publishing Company, 609 Mission Street, San Francisco, California 94105
45. Harvard University Press, Cambridge, Massachusetts 02138
46. D. C. Heath and Company, 1815 Prairie Avenue, Chicago, Illinois 60606
47. Holt, Rinehart, & Winston, Inc., 383 Madison Avenue, New York, New York 10017
48. Houghton Mifflin Company, 110 Tremont Street, Boston, Massachusetts 02107
49. Hubbard Company, P.O. Drawer 100, Defiance, Ohio 43512
50. Indiana University, 200 Pine Hall, Bloomington, Indiana 47401
51. International Reading Association, Box 695, Newark, Delaware 19711
52. Interstate Printers & Publishers, Inc., Danville, Illinois 61832
53. Laidlaw Brothers, of Doubleday & Company, Thatcher & Madison, River Forest, Illinois 60305
54. Lippincott Company, E. Washington Square, Philadelphia, Pennsylvania 19105
55. Little, Brown & Company, 34 Beacon Street, Boston, Massachusetts 02106
56. Lyons and Carnahan, 407 E. 25th Street, Chicago, Illinois 60616
57. Macmillan Company, 434 S. Wabash Avenue, Chicago, Illinois 60605
58. McCormick-Mathers Publishing Co., Box 2212, 1440 E. English Street, Wichita, Kansas 67201
59. McGraw-Hill Book Company, Inc., 330 W. 42nd Street, New York, New York 10036
60. D. McKay Company, Inc., 750 Third Avenue, New York, New York 10017
61. Charles E. Merrill, 1300 Alum Creek Drive, Columbus, Ohio 43216
62. National Council of Teachers of English, 508 S. Sixth Street, Champaign, Illinois 61820

63. National Education Association, 1201 Sixteenth Street N.W., Washington, D.C. (AASA, AERA, ASCD, DCT, EKNE, ESP, NAPSAE, NCSS, NSPRA) 20036
64. National Society for the Study of Education, 5835 Kimbard Avenue, Chicago, Illinois 60637
65. New American Library, 1301 Avenue of the Americas, New York, New York 10019
66. Newark State College, Union, New Jersey 07083
67. W. W. Norton & Company, Inc., 55 Fifth Avenue, New York, New York 10003
68. Oregon State University Press, Corvallis, Oregon 97331
69. Orton Society, Inc., Box 153, Pomfret, Connecticut 06258
70. F. A. Owen Publishing Company, Dansville, New York 14437
71. Sir Issac Pitman & Sons Ltd., Pitman House, Parker Street, Kingsway, London WCZ
72. Plymouth Press, 2921 W. 63rd Street, Chicago, Illinois 60629
73. Pocket Books, Inc., 630 Fifth Avenue, New York, New York 10010
74. Prentice-Hall, Inc., Englewood Cliffs, New Jersey 07632
75. Psychotechnics Press, Psychotechnics, Inc., 1900 Pickwick Avenue, Glenview, Illinois 60025
76. G. P. Putnam and Sons, 200 Madison Avenue, New York, New York 10016
77. Random House, Inc., 501 Madison Avenue, New York, New York 10011
78. Reader's Digest Services, Inc., Educational Division, Pleasantville, New York 10570
79. Rose Education Publishers, 346 Clifton Avenue, Newark, New Jersey 07111
80. Rutgers—The State University, New Brunswick, New Jersey 08903
81. B. H. Sanborn & Company, L. W. Singer Company, 5601 N.W. Highway, Chicago, Illinois 60646
82. Schocken Books, 67 Park Avenue, New York, New York 10016
83. Science Research Associates, Inc., 259 E. Erie Street, Chicago, Illinois 60611
84. Scott, Foresman and Company, 1900 E. Lake Avenue, Glenview, Illinois 60025
85. Charles Scribner's Sons, 597 Fifth Avenue, New York, New York 10017
86. Steck-Vaughn Company, Box 2028, Austin, Texas 78767
87. Superintendent of Documents, U.S. Government Printing Office, Washington, D.C. 20402
88. Syracuse University Press, Box 87, University Station, Syracuse, New York 13210
89. Teachers College Press, Bureau of Publications, 525 W. 129th Street, Columbia University, New York, New York 10027
90. Teachers Publishing Corporation, Darien, Connecticut 06820
91. Treasure Books, Inc., 1107 Broadway, New York, New York 10010

92. United States Department of the Interior, Bureau of Indian Affairs Publications Service, Haskall Institute, Lawrence, Kansas 66044
93. University of Chicago Press, Chicago, Illinois 60634
94. Valparaiso University, Valparaiso, Indiana 46383
95. Webster Division, McGraw-Hill Book Company, Manchester Road, Manchester, Missouri 63011
96. Wisconsin Council of Teachers of English, Wisconsin State University, Oshkosh, Wisconsin 54901

Index